DIVERGENT LIVES

I. VICENTE

DIVERGENT LIVES

Copyright © 2014 I. Vicente

Book edited by Susan Uttendorfsky
Cover design by Stephane Coic, Paris and Mexico City
Photos in the book from author's collection
Formatted by IRONHORSE Formatting

ISBN: 978-0-9916552-3-6

With special thanks to my wife, Estela, for her support in the writing of this book, and for her feedback and insight after reading the first draft; to my sister Susan, for helping to collect pictures and helping me to recall past events to include in the book; to my brother Wil, for taking the time to give me his valuable input for the book; and to my good friends Colin and Judi Reid, and Monica Stomski, for taking the time to read the edited book and provide their valuable critique.

PROLOGUE

It was devastating to see him lying in a coma, with Frankenstein-like staples across two parts of his shaven head. The last time I had seen my older brother, Nelson, was eight years ago at another hospital, Lenox Hill in Manhattan, where our mother was spending a few days with an intestinal problem that required surgery. It seems the only time we run into each other is when we respond to a family emergency. This time it was Nelson who was hospitalized, at the Hospital of Central Connecticut in New Britain, Connecticut. By the time I arrived at the hospital to see him, it was Thursday, February 20, 2014.

He had been taken there the previous Sunday morning after suffering an apparent stroke. Since we had been estranged brothers for many years, my other siblings and parents hesitated to break the news of his health problems to me. I imagine they suspected I wouldn't care. The first one to share the news with me was my other brother, Wil. He is always the peacemaker in the family. He called me on Sunday, February 16th, to let me know Nelson was admitted to the hospital with a stroke. Initially, I was suspicious of the seriousness of Nelson's medical condition, only because he and the family tend to exaggerate matters just to add a dramatic touch to events. I know that stories were customarily embellished in order to give them a higher level of importance, or to make them sound more serious than they actually are, simply to garner the pity of others.

That, however, was not the case this time. By Monday, only a day after Nelson was admitted to the hospital, he was slurring his speech heavily and could not move the left side of his body, literally from head to toes, although he was still alert with his eyes and moving the right side of his body. Sometime that evening, he tried to get up from his bed and fell, hitting his head. This was further complicated by the bleeding of the brain caused by the blood thinner Heparin, routinely administered by his doctors to dissolve a clot found when they did a CT scan and to prevent further blood clotting. By Tuesday, very early in the morning and in the critical care unit, the neurosurgeon performed emergency surgery. He removed the right half of his skull to alleviate the pressure on his brain caused by the bleeding. His brain had swelled considerably and resulted in further damage.

They induced a coma to keep him fully sedated and immobile. Wil called me that morning to let me know Nelson was going into surgery. At that point, I realized we were dealing with a very critical situation. Nelson had several health issues that plagued him before this most recent tragedy. He suffered from Type-1 diabetes, gout, and high blood pressure. Two years ago, he had a defibrillator implanted in his chest to control his heart rate and prevent sudden cardiac arrest. All of this at just fifty-eight years old! I knew that my sister, Susan, was going to the hospital that morning to hold watch over Nelson as he recovered from the brain surgery, so I texted her to get a closer update. Susan has always been very sweet and caring and close to Nelson. She is the one person found at the hospital throughout this ordeal almost on a daily basis, despite the three-hour drive from her Queens, New York, home to the hospital in Connecticut and the fact that she doesn't have a car. She has to rely on her daughter to drive her back and forth.

That Tuesday afternoon, she updated me that Nelson was sedated and resting after surgery. We were all relieved that he had survived the serious surgery. We didn't discuss it, but with his heart condition and high blood pressure, we were quietly concerned that he might not survive. The day before, on Monday, a number of his close friends visited Nelson and apparently became quite emotional at the sight of seeing him unable to speak or move the left side of his body. They were accustomed to seeing him joking, dancing, singing, and living a happy-go-lucky life. He was now in the critical care unit, which requires silence from visitors in order to avoid disturbing the resting patients, but his friends could not control themselves as they cried and prayed for Nelson's rapid recovery. They were prayers that were not to be answered. The doctors and nurses informed the family that he would be sedated in a coma for twenty-four hours, and then be taken off the sedation, whereupon they would observe his responsiveness. Susan was there until early evening, when she passed this update along to me.

The next morning, she checked on his status with the nurses by telephone and learned that he was still sedated and would be taken for a CT scan to check if the swelling in the brain had subsided. If all went well, they would take him off the medication that afternoon. The twenty-four-hour medicated period was due to expire at 2 p.m. Late that afternoon, Susan returned to the hospital to be by his bedside, anticipating that he would wake up and she could breathe a sigh of relief. But she learned from the nurses that the swelling in Nelson's brain had not subsided, and the doctors decided to keep him in the induced coma for another few days.

This was most disappointing and disheartening. It felt, though we would not say it to the whole family openly, that we were losing Nelson. Only Wil and I spoke candidly about thinking that Nelson was unlikely to recover, but not with Susan or my mother. They were hoping and waiting for him to recover, for a miracle, and we didn't want to dampen their hopes. I asked Susan to make sure that, at this critical point, only family members be allowed in to see him and that everyone maintain control and relative quiet when in his room.

The next day, Thursday, Wil and I drove the three and a half hours from our homes in New Jersey to visit Nelson. An update was scheduled in the afternoon from the neurosurgeon who was treating him, and we wanted to be there. When we arrived at 12:30 in the afternoon, we were informed that they had taken Nelson for another CT scan and they would return him to his room in another hour. That news disappointed us on two fronts: we were anxious to see him, and suspected something was wrong for him to require another unscheduled scan. As we waited, we met his wife, Maritza, and their daughter, Angela. It's hard to believe that I had never met them before, but since Nelson and I had been estranged for more than thirty years, I didn't even know where he lived, much less who he was married to and who his children were.

At about 2 p.m. that afternoon, Wil and I were finally able to see Nelson, as the technician and nurse returned him to his room. I was saddened to see him with his head bandaged, a tube in his nose providing oxygen, another one in his mouth to help him breathe, and intravenous tubes in his arms to feed and medicate him. The dismal reality was that he was not able to see or speak with us. In spite of all his faults that resulted in our being estranged, he was always a high-spirited person. Not on this day! I wanted to tell him that I wished we had been better brothers to one another. I wanted to hug him and let him feel how much I truly loved him, despite all of our differences and all of our battles over the years. It was surreal having him in front of me, yet not be able to communicate with him. His body and soul were there, but that was it, at least for now.

As I touched his hand and in a whispered voice asked him to hang in there, I returned to my memories of the way we grew up.

CHAPTER ONE

The First Son

Nelson was born on July 11, 1955, at Saint Francis Hospital in the South Bronx to our mother, Julia Victoria Vicente de Marrero and her estranged husband, Benjamin Marrero. She was eighteen years old when she gave birth to her first son. They lived in the South Bronx, New York, not far from the Beck Street home where Victoria grew up after the family emigrated from Puerto Rico nine years earlier. In 1946, Julio Vicente, the family patriarch, arrived in New York City with a brother-in-law, Flor Soto. He found work at a pillow factory in the Bronx and sent for the rest of the family a few years later.

Benjamin was accustomed to living the life of a single guy, hanging out in bars with women. Victoria was young in years, as well as in life experience, having lived a sheltered life as a young girl in Guayama, a small rural town located about 56 miles south of the big city of San Juan, Puerto Rico. She was just sixteen years old when she and Benjamin were married. Marriage didn't alter Benjamin's lifestyle, and while Victoria was pregnant with Nelson, they separated. She went back to her parents' home and Nelson was born while she lived there. As the oldest surviving child of what would be fifteen children, she helped care for her brothers and sisters, and her own child.

Victoria's youngest sister, Milagros, was born at about the same time as Nelson, which meant that she had two infants to care for as her mother, Domitila, was busy with the other growing children and the home. Julio, the proud patriarch of the family, somehow made ends meet by working long hours. He was industrious, responsible, and proud. Four of the fifteen children died in early infancy in Guayama, leaving a family of eleven children and one grandchild. As the summer of 1955 came to an end, Victoria met a young man, Israel, who was twenty-four years old at the time, while she was still eighteen. He was a timid man who was born in Mayaguez, Puerto Rico, on the west coast of the island, and immigrated to New York at the age of fifteen in 1946 to live with an aunt in the South Bronx. Two years later, he enlisted in the Army. He served for three years during the Korean War and was deployed abroad in Pusan, Korea, for one year and three days, where hard-pressed American, South Korean and United Nations forces were desperately hanging onto the southeast tip of the Korean peninsula. Israel was trained as a Medical Technician and, when deployed, became a member of Medical Detachment 704, for which he proudly earned a Combat Medical Badge. He was awarded the CMB for his service in accompanying infantrymen into the Demilitarized Zone (DMZ) between North and South Korea. He was also decorated with the

Korean Presidential Citation and the Korean Service Medal.

He had been out of the military for four years and was working at a factory that printed history books when he met Victoria. Julio forbade his daughters from going out without a chaperone, and she had an infant child to care for, so Israel visited the house at 949 Hoe Avenue and chatted with her outside on the stoop. It was important to Victoria that Israel liked her child. She was interested in starting a life and growing a family. Disappointed and sad that her marriage to Benjamin had fallen apart, she did not want that to happen again. Israel lived nearby on Dawson Street with his aunt, Lucy, and sometimes visited Victoria's house in the evening while the family was asleep, hoping he could speak with her in private outside. Her father, Julio, who was a friendly man, but equally hot-tempered, occasionally chased him away. Israel was known to throw pebbles at Victoria's bedroom window to awaken her and let her know he was outside, hoping she would come out to speak with him. It angered her father, but aroused laughter among her younger siblings.

The sisters, and even her mother, Domitila, began referring to Israel as Brown. Everyone had a nickname at the house, and as a sign of acceptance into the family, Brown was the one he was titled with. It was an affectionate and comical name affixed to him for seemingly always wearing a brown suit when he went by the house to visit. Once a nickname was chosen for someone in the family, the person's birth-given name was surely never uttered again. Victoria was Vicky, Israel was Brown, and Nelson was Puchi, a name known as a term of affection for an infant who was skinny. Puchi had a resemblance to his young mother, but also to his father.

Nelson, as Vicky's first son and Julio and Domitila's first grandson, was naturally adored by all in the family.

Israel and Victoria moved in together to a small room they rented a block away from her parents' home. Ironically, her maiden name and his last name were identical—Vicente—so she didn't have to get accustomed to a new last name if they got married. Over the years, people have wondered what relation they had to each other prior to being married to merit having the same last name. But it was simply and purely coincidental, perhaps a twist of fate. Just nine days before Puchi's second birthday, Victoria gave birth to me, her second child and Israel's first. They named me Israel Jr. (Junior), after my dad. The family tradition of picking a nickname for everyone, and my bulbous baby figure, served as the inspiration for them to assign me the unofficial name of Fatty.

From the beginning of their relationship, Israel proudly behaved as if Nelson was his child. He embraced the responsibility and always treated him as his own. It was as if I was his second son and Nelson his first. Victoria was officially divorced from Benjamin, but did not marry Israel until 1961, as they were about to bring their fourth child into the world.

CHAPTER TWO

Intervale Avenue

With the family growing quickly, they moved into a two-bedroom apartment on the third floor of a five-story building just a half block from the Intervale Avenue subway station. While he worked at his factory job to support the family, she stayed at home caring for the children and the home. The Intervale apartment saw the family grow to include five children. In the early years, Puchi and I grew up together as close as two brothers could be. Mom always made sure we were clean and neatly dressed when we went out. There were many families with children of our age on the block, so there was plenty of opportunity for playing and making friends. I was the stockier kid and more athletic, while Puchi was small, skinny, and not interested in sports. He was more interested in mischief around the apartment. Evelyn was born in August of 1959, so Mom was busy with three children to care for.

When Nelson and I were not watching cartoons or a show on TV, we were around the kitchen while Mom prepared dinner. She was an excellent cook and the entire apartment lit up with the fragrance of cilantro and *sofrito*, a blended mix of aromatic spices used in many Puerto Rican dishes. She used them in preparing beans, rice, beef stew, or pork chops, and other dishes. The beans and stews always included *aceitunas*, or olives. Sometimes she used the pitted olives stuffed with red peppers, sometimes it was the olives with the pits in them. Those were slightly less expensive than the pitted ones.

One late afternoon while watching *Dennis the Menace*, we joined Mom in the kitchen as she prepared dinner. I always asked her for a taste of whatever she was preparing that was ready to eat. Sometimes it was a spoonful of beans or stew, or a slice of *platano maduro*, fried sweet plantain.

One particular afternoon, I was sampling the *aceitunas*. We went back to the living room to watch the TV while I chewed my olive. Puchi, who was five years old at the time, while I was three, suggested that I put the pit of the olive in my nose. After I had eaten the olive and scraped the pit clean with my teeth, I placed it in my right nostril. Puchi wanted to see if I could then remove it easily, so he asked me to take it out. He was not interested in trying that on himself, so why not his younger, curious brother?

As I put my two fingers in my nostril, I felt relieved that I could grab the edge of the olive pit. It felt that I was about to pull it out, so all was good. Just as the pit was easing out, my fingers lost their grip and the pit moved back in. At that point, I started to get scared. I tried to remove the pit one more time, but again it slipped back in, seemingly deeper into my nostril. I was afraid that it would go way up in my nose and do some harm to me; maybe I wouldn't be able to breathe. I was born asthmatic, so the prospect of not being able to breathe was scary to me. I panicked and ran into the kitchen to tell Mom what had happened. She tried, but was unable to remove the pit from my nose. Probably tweezers would have done the trick, but it didn't occur to her to try that.

She stopped her cooking and took Puchi and me to the Emergency Room at Prospect Hospital. The ER doctor was able to remove the pit with tweezers. He pressed one edge of the tweezers on the outside of my nose to prevent the pit from moving while he grabbed it with another pair. In a matter of seconds, the pit was out, and I felt relieved that I did not feel any pain in the process. We returned home and Mom resumed her cooking.

Unbelievably, as Puchi and I played in and around the kitchen, still eating *aceitunas*, he convinced me to try the pit-in-the-nose trick one more time. Listening to my older brother, I did just that. There we were on our way to the Emergency Room at Prospect hospital one more time. The ER doctor could not believe it when he saw us and learned that we did it again! This time we all knew the routine, so I got into position on the stretcher and waited for him to pull out the pit. On the way home, my mom made a stop at a Dunkin Donuts and bought us some donuts, making Puchi and I promise that we would not insert any more olive pits inside my nose. She was twenty-four years old at the time and quite patient with us, considering that we interrupted her cooking not once, but twice.

One year, Puchi and I were invited to a Halloween party at a neighbor's home up the street from us. Puchi was seven years old and I was five. Mom dressed us neatly for the party. Since it was a party, she didn't think we needed Halloween costumes. We were quite fine with that and didn't protest. The host of the party had set up games to keep us entertained. In addition to pin-the-tail – on-the-donkey, playing musical chairs, and eating Cheetos and drinking juice and soda, they set up a tin tub with water and filled it with apples. Each of us had a certain amount of time to duck our heads in the tub and grab an apple with our teeth. We had to hold our arms behind our backs as we bent over to bob in the water.

I had a competitive streak in me, and was excited to get to my turn. When I ducked my head in the water and felt an apple on my mouth, I realized that my missing front teeth were a handicap. I pushed the apple so it turned and brought the stem close to my mouth, but even then, I was unable to grab it. I didn't have sufficient traction with my teeth to bite the apple, either. I bobbed my head up a few times to catch my breath before trying again, but each attempt proved fruitless. Puchi came to my rescue when he successfully grabbed an apple and handed it to me.

On our way to our apartment after the party, just down the block, we were chased by a dog. We were afraid it would bite one of us or both, so we hurried inside the entrance door to our building. The door was made of heavy iron and glass, and the dog was caught in the door as it closed when he tried to get inside, presumably to bite us. I felt bad that the dog was caught in the door, because I heard it whimper as it pulled its head out from the door, turned, and walked away. But I was glad that we were safe inside our building.

Puchi and I often got into mischief in the neighborhood, including the time that I scraped my entire face on the sidewalk. We were with some friends who had found the frame of a supermarket shopping cart. We didn't know how the basket was removed or who removed it, but the kids were using the frame as a vehicle to ride down the street for joy. The street we were playing on was downhill, and provided the perfect angle to thrust the cart down the hill, picking up speed on the way down.

As was usual for me back then, I volunteered to be the first one to ride. I sat on the cart and one of the kids gave a slight shove to get me started. I began to pick up speed as I was propelled forward. Unexpectedly, there was a part of the sidewalk's concrete that was raised—I guess from normal wear and tear—though I didn't know it at the time. The front wheels of the cart collided with the bump in the sidewalk and, as the cart's momentum was abruptly interrupted, I was catapulted forward as if I was shot out of a cannon.

I flew forward and landed face-first on the sidewalk, scraping my bouncing face on the rough concrete until my body finally came to a stop. I was crying and in great pain as Puchi helped me upstairs to our apartment. With scrapes on my forehead, chin, nose, and cheeks, my mom cleaned the wounds and consoled me.

Whenever one of us got hurt, she tried to ease our pain with a treat, just as she did when she got us Dunkin Donuts after the second *aceituna* trip to the hospital. This time she gave me a piece of watermelon, which was one of my favorite fruits. I enjoyed all fruits, especially watermelon, mangoes, and quenepas, the tropical fruit we used to get from Puerto Rico. As soon as I touched the watermelon with my mouth, I screamed. The raw wounds around my nose and chin touched the watery fruit, causing a burning sensation. I told Mom I could not eat the watermelon, so she cut it into small pieces to make it easier for me to pick up with a fork and eat it that way. Still, I felt too exhausted to want to eat it. I just wanted the pain to go away.

Puchi was with me, but I don't think he had any intention of riding that cart down the hill. I was the more adventurous brother, and consequently the one who was frequently injured. Puchi encouraged me, the younger brother, to attempt things that he knew he would not do himself. Even among the other friends who were with us, I was the guinea pig who test drove the cart down the hill.

After school, we always walked home together while Mom waited for us at the door to our apartment. She would prepare a snack for us, usually cookies and milk. We watched *Popeye the Sailor* and *The Flintstones* while we ate our snack. For a few days, our routine was interrupted by a frightening scene Puchi and I endured as we climbed the stairs to our third floor apartment. On the first day of this episode, as we got home from school, Mom was by the stairs on the third floor yelling, "Fatty, Puchi, stay down there. Don't come up yet."

We could hear other neighbors outside of their apartments on both the second and third floors. Some were talking to each other, and some were yelling to another neighbor, Sonia, trying to convince her to go inside her apartment. Sonia, who lived on the second floor with her husband, Roberto, was screaming while wielding a knife in her right hand. As Puchi and I walked gingerly up the stairs halfway up to the second floor, I could see her outside her corner apartment. We were scared, but curious. Nothing that Sonia was yelling was intelligible to me or Nelson, but we were frightened that she would harm us if we walked up to the second floor.

None of the other neighbors—all women who stayed home with their children while their husbands worked—felt safe enough to approach Sonia to calm her down. It seemed that Sonia could not even hear them asking her to go back into her apartment. She was standing to the right of the staircase, and we had to go to the left side to continue up to the third floor. I thought that if Puchi and I could get to the second floor landing, we could run past Sonia and up to our floor. Since she wasn't moving from in front of her apartment door, as if she was guarding it against a potential intruder, we could get by her and not be harmed. With the neighbors and Mom speaking to Sonia to distract her, we worked up the courage to run up the stairs. As we got to the second floor, a chill raced through my body as Sonia kept screaming at no one in particular.

This went on for two more days, until Roberto stopped by our apartment to talk to my mom.

"*Sonia se me enfermo y la tuve que dejar en el hospital,*" he told her.

Although he said Sonia got sick and he had to have her hospitalized, my mom knew that Sonia had gone crazy and that he put her in an asylum. We never saw her in the building again after that.

By this time, Mom was pregnant again and expecting her fourth child that winter. My uncle, Wilfredo, who was one year younger than dad, had come to visit. He asked his brother to let him stay with us for a while. The way it was explained to us years later, Wilfredo had gotten involved with some unsavory characters and was into drugs. Dad felt he had a bigger responsibility to protect his pregnant wife and three children, so he declined his brother's request to stay with us. As it was, we only had a two-bedroom apartment. Puchi, Evelyn—who was nicknamed Tata—and I shared one bedroom, and my parents the other. A few weeks later, Wilfredo was murdered. I'm sure my dad felt terrible and second-guessed his decision not to help his brother. But he had to protect his wife and kids. That November, Mom gave birth to her fourth child, another son, and named him Wilfredo after my uncle.

CHAPTER THREE

Mayaguez

Wilfredo was born a chubby baby and so was nicknamed Chubby. All of us, except for Puchi, were chubby babies at birth, so it was as if Mom and Dad were running out of nicknames. We all could have been named Fatty or Chubby.

Approximately a year after Chubby was born, in late 1962, Mom was pregnant with what would be her fifth and last child. I can almost remember when it happened. One afternoon as us kids were watching TV and playing in the living room, I decided to walk around. I made my way to the kids' bedroom door. As I opened the door, I saw Dad on top of Mom with the covers over them. He raised and turned his head toward me, but didn't say anything. I quickly closed the door and turned back into the living room. I never asked them what they were doing and they just let it go as well. That was the only time that I walked in on my mom and dad, thank goodness!

As Mom's belly got bigger and bigger, she and Dad decided that since this was going to be their last child, it would be nice if the baby was born in their native land. Very much attached to their Puerto Rican culture, they wanted to have at least this last child born in either Mom's town of Guayama, or Dad's town of Mayaguez. They decided that since Dad's parents had a bigger house than Mom's relatives, and were our only grandparents living on the island, that was where the baby would be born. About two weeks before the baby was due to be born, in late May of 1963, my mom packed the four of us up and we headed to John F. Kennedy Airport to board a flight to San Juan. My dad took us to the airport, but stayed behind to work.

It was the very first airplane trip for the kids, and we were excited. Puchi and I were the oldest, so we helped Mom carry bags and watch Tata and Chubby. Mom was very pregnant, so she was unable to carry too much. Puchi and I repeatedly switched sitting in the window and middle seat so we could look out the window. I wanted to see how the men below loaded the luggage while we sat at the gate. As we were about to take off, Mom made the sign of the cross on her head and chest, said, "God bless you" to us, and closed her eyes. I was just excited to hear the roar of the plane as we took off. I couldn't believe that we were on an airplane and flying through the air. The best part was when they brought us a meal. We were eating on a plane while flying through the air. They even gave us silverware to eat with. After we finished our meal, I put the silverware in one of our bags we had placed underneath our seats as a souvenir of our trip.

It was the end of May and the weather in New York City was warm, but when we landed in San Juan, I felt a different kind of heat. The air felt moist and much hotter. We were all excited to be in a different place and hurried with Mom to get to the car waiting for us. My grandfather, Eleodoro, and grandmother, Ernestina, whom we called Abuelo and Abuela, had someone pick us up at the airport. We loaded our luggage into the trunk and eagerly bounced into the car. I had never seen palm trees before, not even in books. As we drove what seemed to be all day from San Juan to Mayaguez, we saw palm trees everywhere. Every now and then, we saw chickens and roosters on the side of a road. In the Bronx, there were people selling coconut and pineapple ices in small, white pleated cups. The man selling them would scoop the ice and fill the paper cup. Others sold *piraguas*, shaved ice crammed into a cone-shaped paper cup with sweet syrup poured over the ice. There were many flavors to choose from—cherry, grape, coconut, tamarind, and others. Mom would buy us one whenever we were out around Southern Boulevard shopping. My favorite was always the coconut ice or the tamarind *piragua*. Puchi and I gravitated to the tropical flavors, for sure.

I always wondered where the people got the idea to set up these carts in the streets of the Bronx. Driving along the streets in Puerto Rico, my curiosity was satisfied. Since I could see the same type of carts in Puerto Rico from which men or women sold tropical ices, or *piraguas*, I assumed that is where it all came from. In any case, I couldn't wait until we got to Abuela's house so Puchi and I could go outside and find an ice or *piragua* cart in town.

Finally, after the long drive that must have taken four hours, we arrived at Abuela and Abuelo's house. Their house was on a dead end street, on the left side. It was the next to last house near the dead end. The last house on the street was a large ranch enclosed by a rickety gate. The road on the block was gravel and there was no marked parking available. People parked in front of their homes as close as possible, so other neighbors' cars could get by. Their house was walking distance to the center of town, which was good for Puchi and me. We could easily walk to town to get a coconut ice. Abuelo and Abuela greeted us with a kiss and a hug and helped us get settled inside.

They had a pretty nice house. The entrance had a chain-link fence that led to a porch. The fence allowed them to keep the front door open to get air circulation in the constant heat. They had fans to deal with the heat, but no air conditioning. From the front door, you entered directly into the living room, where the furniture was rich, dark wood with cane seats and backs. All the tabletops, including the dining table, had cream-colored lace linens. Thankfully, the furniture was not covered in skin-sticking plastic, like ours was at home. Near the entrance was a rocking chair that only Abuela sat on.

My aunt, Jeannette, lived in the house with my grandparents. Occasionally, back home, I heard Mom and Dad wondering out loud when, if ever, Jeannette was going to get married. She seemed to be devoted to her parents, though, and remained single all her life. As soon as we put our things away in our room, Puchi and I went outside to play. Initially, we stayed close by and just hung out on the porch. We were looking down the street as if letting the neighborhood know the kids from New York had arrived. I sat on the porch at the entrance gate and slid my legs through the bottom of the fence so they were hanging out on the other side. The homes on the block were on short stilts, so I could put my legs down on the other side without touching the ground. Puchi was standing next to me, when suddenly, across the street I saw a giant rat running across the bottom of a neighbor's house. A chill ran through my body and I quickly pulled my legs inside the porch, scratching both with the sharp ends of the fence.

Even though it hurt, I didn't make a fuss about it and didn't tell Mom. I didn't want to let anyone know, especially Abuela, that we barely arrived and I already managed to be injured. Besides, it was not nearly as painful as the time I scraped my entire face on the sidewalk. I don't think Puchi even noticed, either, which was good, because he might have run to Mom and told her. My biggest fear, though, was that rat. Now I was afraid that we would be attacked by rats in the night while we slept. Abuela's house was pretty clean and tidy, so I had nothing to fear, except that after seeing that rat outside, my imagination was running away with me.

Mayaguez has always been known as, among other things, the City of the Mango. I'm not sure why, since there are mangoes all over the island. What I did notice was that, just inside the entrance to the ranch at the end of the block, there was a huge mango tree. Puchi and I walked over there and I could tell that we could easily open the rickety gate and get inside. Once we got inside the property, we saw mangoes up in the huge tree and on the ground. The ones that had fallen from the tree must have been very sweet, I thought. We didn't want any neighbor to see us for fear that they would tell Abuela and she would scold us, or worse, tell Mom. So, as Puchi watched at the gate, I ran under the tree and picked up two mangoes, one for each of us. All of a sudden, a lady began screaming at me from the front porch of the house. Conveniently for us, she was about one hundred feet away. She was screaming for us to get out and leave her mangoes alone. The house was too far away for her to get to us, but she frightened us anyway. I ran out with the two mangoes and no one at Abuela's house ever found out.

My feeling was that the fallen mangoes were only going to rot, and more would keep falling. The tree was huge and filled with them, so what harm was there in us taking a couple and enjoying them? With that reasoning, Puchi and I went back daily during our visit to Abuela's. Each time, the lady screamed at us, but she never left her balcony. It became almost comical—she knew we were going to take some mangoes, and we knew she would scream, but would not come down from her perch on the porch.

At night, we all slept in beds with mosquito nets over them to keep the bugs from biting us while we slept. Puchi and I shared a bed, and Tata and Chubby in another with Mom. She had to be careful that one of the kids didn't kick her belly. We heard the coqui tree frogs singing at night, along with other creatures, like lizards and cats. The first night we slept there, Puchi scared the daylights out of me. We could see lizards crawling on the screen of the open window near us. Puchi rubbed my leg with his foot to mimic a lizard crawling on me. I almost jumped out of the bed!

Each morning, we woke up to the sound of crowing roosters and the strong, fragrant smell of Puerto Rican coffee brewing in Abuela's kitchen. Even though the house was small, there was a sense of tranquility to be in a different place. And I enjoyed my early morning walks with Abuelo to the town bakery to pick up a fresh loaf of bread for our breakfast. Glaucoma had stolen Abuelo's eyesight, but he knew the town he lived in all his life and could easily make it on his own to the bakery. He didn't even walk with a cane! Although I was walking to the bakery with him when we were there, some kids in the neighborhood would still approach him, take him by the hand, and accompany him to the bakery. There was something about experiencing that walk with Abuelo and witnessing how kindly the people in town and in the bakery treated him that left an indelibly positive impression on me as a kid. The people were happy to see Eleodoro and eager to help him walk to and from town.

Eleodoro Vicente was born on December 1, 1898, in Mayaguez, Puerto Rico. His mother, Antonia Campos, was born in Puerto Rico and married Santiago Vicente, who was born in Spain. They had four children, two boys and two girls. Eleodoro was the second child, two years younger than Ernesto, followed by Lucy, three years later, and Gladys, two years after her. Eleodoro was only five years old, and Ernesto only seven, when their father died and left Antonia a widow with four children to care for. Consequently, Ernesto and Eleodoro, as the "men" in the family, never went to school, and instead helped their mother make sure there was food on the table for the family, while the girls attended school.

Little Eleodoro learned to do carpentry work to help maintain their small house in Mayaguez. When he was a bit older, he started working in a local store, called a *Pulperia*, the name given to nineteenth-century grocery stores in rural towns of Puerto Rico and other Latin American countries. These stores sold everything from tobacco and cigars to groceries. The skills he learned working there, and the carpentry he taught himself out of necessity, became his traits for most of his life. That is, until glaucoma robbed him completely of his eyesight. Eleodoro was in his early thirties when he married Ernestina Mas, and she became Ernestina Mas de Vicente. Ernestina was thirteen years younger than he was. They had five children and lived in the same house in Mayaguez all of their lives. That house today is still in the family, almost a century later, as Jeannette, who never married, continues to live there. An uncle, Edwin, lives across the street, and another uncle, Papo, whose real name is Rafael, lives a few blocks away.

Abuelo and I returned home from the bakery with a large loaf of hot, crispy bread. We all sat around the dining table near the living room dunking pieces of bread into cups of coffee sweetened with enough sugar to sweeten the bread, which was crispy on the outside and soft and doughy on the inside. Puchi and I had bread and coffee, and Tata and Chubby had cereal with milk.

I was excited that we were in Puerto Rico and that we would have a sister or brother born there. Mom was getting close to her time to give birth, when something happened that changed everything. One afternoon, I was out on the porch and overheard her arguing with Abuela. I wasn't sure what the argument was about. I knew that Abuela could be grumpy and repeatedly reminded us not to flush the toilet if we just peed. That helped her minimize water usage and hence, the cost they incurred. I thought that might have finally aggravated Mom, who was sensitive and irritable in the late stages of her pregnancy, but I wasn't sure that was the cause. All I did know is that Mom came out onto the porch and told us to pack up, that we were leaving. Mom could be impulsive, and she didn't hesitate.

She packed up all our things, and just that quickly she arranged for us to be on a flight back home. She hired a car to take us to the airport, and that same evening, we were back in the Bronx. She didn't even take the time to inform Dad that we were coming home. We arrived at the apartment in a taxi from JFK Airport. She put the key in the door and we surprised Dad as he was sitting in the living room watching the Yankees game on TV. He was shocked that we were home so soon and the baby was not even born yet. Mom explained to him that she had an argument with Abuela and decided to return home. I suppose she gave him a more detailed account of what occurred when we were in bed and out of listening range.

A week later on June 15, 1963, we had a baby sister, Susan, born in Lenox Hill Hospital, the same one where I was born. We were able to see her when Mom and Dad brought her home from the hospital. I remember that Mom placed Susan on her bed while she put away some of her things. I was standing there, admiring the new baby, when she moved and almost fell off the edge of the bed. I was able to grab her quickly before she fell and placed her in the center of the bed, away from the edge. I watched her until Mom came and picked her up to put her in the crib that was in the corner of their bedroom by the window. Susan was the only one of the five of us who was never assigned a nickname, other than having her name shortened to Susie. She was a chubby baby as well, but apparently all the synonyms for that word they could think of had already been used up.

One afternoon as Puchi and I got home from school, we found a chaotic scene. My grandmother, Domitila, was there with my aunt, Irma, and Mom was crying hysterically. A man had tried to attack her in the hallway as she arrived home with the other kids. She was inconsolable and afraid to stay there. Abuela insisted that she move from that apartment. That very afternoon, while Dad was still at work, Abuela decided that Tata and I would go stay with her while Mom and Irma took Puchi, Chubby, and Susan to look for a new apartment for us. I started crying because I didn't want to go with Abuela and wanted to be with Mom. I went with her anyway, but was not happy about it, and cried the entire way to her house.

We lived in that apartment for a while longer before we were able to move out, but Mom was always extra careful when going out or coming back home. One afternoon, though, she went to a neighbor's apartment for a brief visit. She took Puchi, Chubby and Tata, but left me in the apartment alone watching Susan, who was in her crib. She instructed me on how to lock the door, including securing the thick, solid steel bar that plugged into a plate on the floor that was made of the same steel. The other end latched into another plate on the door. That was a common security measure in Bronx apartments, designed to keep burglars from breaking down the front door. She also instructed me not to open the door for any stranger. I was afraid and hoped she would come back quickly. I must have turned white as a ghost when I heard someone knock on the door. I walked slowly to the door and asked who it was. I shouldn't have spoken, because I wasn't supposed to let anyone know that I was home alone, but I thought that maybe it was Mom.

When I heard a man's voice respond to my question, I panicked and ran back into my parents' bedroom. Mom and Dad had a tall dresser with legs that raised the body off the floor. I was so scared that I slid underneath the dresser to hide. I was sweating and nervous as I sat there, crouched in a fetal position. A frantic chill came over my body when I heard someone jangling keys to try to open the door. I imagined a man getting into the apartment and taking me away, or killing me. I came out from under the dresser only when I heard Mom's voice inside the apartment. It wasn't until years later that I wondered why I was left alone in the first place.

CHAPTER FOUR

Tremont

Sometime after that frightening experience, we moved to 179th Street near Tremont Avenue. The two-bedroom apartment on the second floor of a building was directly across the street from Mom's good friend, Julia. Julia and her husband, Manny, had two daughters, Daisy and Nancy, who were about the same ages as Puchi and I. We spent many evenings at their apartment on weekends at the parties they had with close friends. We didn't have many parties at our apartment for some reason, but Julia and Manny loved having people over. They spent the time listening to Latin music—mostly boleros—drinking beer, rum and coke, and sharing stories. The kids gradually gravitated to the girls' bedroom to play games. One of our favorites was Spin the Bottle. I had a crush on Daisy, so I made sure that each time it was my turn to spin, the mouth of the bottle would point to her, or close enough to her, that I got to kiss her on the cheek. My plans didn't help too much, though, because it turned out she had a crush on Puchi, so she didn't pay attention to me. Nancy had a crush on me, but I didn't like her, so I never paid attention to her.

One Halloween, Puchi and I were going trick or treating in the neighborhood. We tried to have very different costumes every year, but that one year, I thought his costume was very strange, although it wasn't his idea. My costume that year was Halloween paint on my face and a long sock filled with chalk. I turned the chalk into dust by slamming the sock against the sidewalk or a building's brick façade. I then marked the buildings as Puchi and I walked around asking for treats. Mom decided that she would dress Puchi in a costume using girls' clothing. She put makeup all over his face, a dress, and shoes. He went out on Halloween looking like a girl. I remember thinking that it was bizarre walking the streets with my brother looking like that, even if it was Halloween. In retrospect, it was an example of how much Mom loved and favored Puchi because he was her first son and the one who most resembled her. My other siblings were too young to go out on Halloween with us, so it was just Puchi and me. The people whose apartments we visited asking for treats were amused by his costume. The women especially commented on how cute he looked. They hardly noticed I was there. It didn't bother me as long as I got some treats, but looking back on that experience, it began to plant the seeds in shaping my own future. It also planted the seeds in Puchi for his. His joy, his reward, came from being noticed and applauded. He didn't need the candy or the coins.

While Mom was visibly happy and proud that Puchi looked like a miniature version of her—that he looked like her daughter and not her son—Puchi just seemed to glow in the attention that everyone paid to him. In fact, in subsequent years, he didn't even go out on Halloween with me, while I was always preparing for that rewarding day, forecasting what I could bring home. Every year I went from building to building, visiting all the apartments, and even stopping people in the street asking, "Trick or treat?" One year I went to the Tremont Avenue train station at 5 p.m. with black and white paint on my face to ask for treats as people were coming home from work. My inspiration to venture down there came from a TV commercial I had seen the day before. It was a commercial for UNICEF, an organization I was too young to know anything about. In the commercial, they were promoting kids trick or treating for UNICEF by going out into their communities and repeating those words. The commercial depicted adults smiling as they willingly gave the kids money as treats. I learned years later that what UNICEF expected was for those kids to then donate that money to its organization.

At six, seven, and even eight years old, I missed that part.

I simply felt that if people coming home from work would be so willing to accommodate a kid standing at the foot of the train station by giving him coins on Halloween, I should add that venue to my list of stops, along with all the apartment buildings in the neighborhood. I didn't give much thought to the possibility that I would meet some of the same people when I visited the apartment buildings later that evening. A feeling of guilt came over me years later when I learned that I was supposed to send the money I made at the train station to UNICEF, but I didn't even know how to do that.

Christmas at home was always festive, with the tradition of Mom putting up the tree that we helped decorate. Although we were poor, Mom and Dad always managed to have presents for us. In the 1960s, well before the advent of first generation computer games such as Pac-Man, it was fairly easy to please us kids with almost anything. A game of "Operation" or "Trouble," or a box of miniature toy soldiers, maybe a tea set or doll for the girls, was all we needed. Our apartment was too small for my parents to hide the gifts, and there were five kids. I remember one Christmas time when I opened a closet and saw an unwrapped box of toy soldiers, complete with a fort. Mom told me that it was for someone else and that Santa Claus would be bringing our toys. But I really liked toy soldiers, so I cried and cried until she caved, or so I thought, and decreed that I could have it at Christmas. It wasn't until I stopped believing in Santa Claus that I realized it was destined for me all along.

One Christmas, Puchi and I were able to get an extra gift each by walking past the police precinct on Tremont Avenue. We were frequently outside, hanging out in the neighborhood, and one day around Christmas time, we walked up Tremont Avenue just looking at stores with their holiday lights blinking and tinsel shining in the windows. As we approached the precinct, a police officer invited us inside and offered us each a wrapped gift from their Toys for Tots box that was sitting in a corner just inside the station. Puchi and I picked the largest box we could carry and went directly home to show Mom what the nice officer had given us.

Once we started going to school, Puchi and I began using our given names and dropped the Puchi and Fatty. We were now to be known as Nelson and Israel. It was a natural transition, since all our school registration information only had our real names. We still used the nicknames at home—at least for a while longer—but never outside the house. We never went to kindergarten; each of us started school from the first grade. Nelson was just one year ahead of me, so he started school at P.S. 6 on Tremont Avenue before me. Once he started going to school, carrying his small book bag and dressed in a shirt and clip-on tie, I was anxious for my turn to come.

The next year, I joined Nelson at P.S. 6. When the weather was nice, we got to the schoolyard early in the morning, met up with friends, and played until the bell sounded for us to line up to enter the building. Most of the boys played punch ball; the girls either double-dutch or hopscotch. Nelson wasn't too interested in sports, so he stood around and watched while I played. One of the favorite things to do while playing punch ball was to hit the ball over the wall of a short section of the building. It was slightly more than a story tall, maybe twelve feet high. If someone hit the ball over that wall and it stayed on its roof, it counted as a home run. The best part, though, was that one of the kids had to climb up to the roof to retrieve the ball. It seemed that everyone wanted a turn at doing the climb to that roof, except for me. I wasn't at all excited about risking a fall from that height.

One thing Nelson liked to do was visit our grandparents on Hoe Avenue. He was a favorite of all our aunts and uncles, and our grandmother. Sometimes in the summer months, he and I would go to their house by walking from our apartment. The walk from our home to theirs was about ten blocks, or two subway stops from Tremont Avenue to Freeman Street. About halfway into our walk one day, we came upon a street fair with amusement park rides. Puchi wanted to go on one of the rides.

"Let's get on one ride before we go to Abuela's. I have some money."

I didn't mind, so we went into the fair and the first ride that was in front of us was the Zero Gravity ride. It raises and tilts at an angle as it spins around faster and faster while you stand straight up strapped in your assigned spot. It spins around so fast that your body is stuck in place and you are unable to move at all. As I tried to stick my head out the force created by the spinning, it pulled my head back. It wasn't until the ride was over that I realized that Nelson had gotten sick and threw up. We both came off the ride dizzy, wobbling until we regained our balance. Since the force of the ride had my head plastered to the back wall, I could not notice that he had gotten sick. He had to walk the rest of the way to Abuela's house with his shirt and pants stained. Once we got to the house, Abuela washed his clothes and we went outside to play.

When Nelson was ten years old and I was eight, he had a girlfriend in the neighborhood named Rosita. She had recently arrived with her family from Puerto Rico and did not speak English. She was lanky and thin with light brown skin and long dark brown hair that her mom always put in a ponytail. I didn't find her particularly pretty, and thought it was odd that she didn't speak English. Rosita often asked Nelson to buy her candy at the store that was then on Tremont Avenue and Vyse Avenue, where we had moved to from 179th Street. That apartment was much closer to our school. Rosita used to get angry when Nelson did not comply with her request to buy her something at the candy store. I thought she had broken her elbow one day when just a few yards between the store and our apartment she bent down on the sidewalk, banged her elbow on the concrete, and shouted to me that "*¡Nelson es duro, duro, duro!*" symbolizing that he was as hard with money as her elbow hitting the concrete. Her demonstration both surprised and scared me. I was certain she had broken her elbow as hard as she hit it on the ground several times. I don't know why she thought that he would have money to buy her anything, or that he should.

Perhaps Rosita thought that with Nelson's job at the *bodega* on Tremont Avenue, he would have money to be able to spend some on his girlfriend. But even at that early age, Nelson was not one to treat his girlfriend lavishly. It was a trait I saw manifest itself over the subsequent years as we grew into adolescents and adults. The job Nelson had at the *bodega* was his first job. Proud that my brother had a job, I walked into the *bodega* to see him sweeping the floor or stocking the fridge with sodas and beer. In retrospect, it was around this time when I began to see how different he and I were growing up to be.

It was at this *bodega* that Nelson, beginning to show an imprudent nature, grabbed a bag of cash that the owner had placed on a shelf behind the counter. If his impulsive decision was, at least subconsciously, a test to see if he could get away with it, what ensued did not portend good things. Nelson abruptly stopped working at the *bodega*. He simply did not show up anymore. He did not inform the owner of his decision, and he did not give our parents a reason, either. He and I were very close, so my inquisitive nature made me wonder why he had stopped working there, which I enviously saw as a cool job. It just didn't make any sense to me. My curiosity antenna went up as I was determined to uncover the unanswered question—why did Nelson quit his first job so suddenly?

My parents did not question Nelson, so after a few days, he felt the coast was clear. One afternoon, he came home with a stack of toys. When Mom asked him where he got the toys from, Nelson was ready with a convincingly well-thought-out answer. He told her that a friend's mother had taken both of them shopping on her son's birthday and bought him all the toys as a gift.

"That was so nice of her to do. I would like to meet her," Mom responded. "Ask her when I can meet her to thank her."

Nelson told her that he would arrange for them to meet. Dad was working and got home late at night, and had other priorities that preoccupied him, such as feeding a family of seven on a factory salary, so he left these sorts of details to Mom. Mom waited for Nelson to set up the meeting with the lady, but it was scheduled and canceled twice. According to Nelson, the lady injured her foot after slamming her car door on it and had to go to the hospital with a broken foot. Somehow, Mom was not suspicious, but I certainly was!

As Mom forgot about the requested meeting, Nelson realized an important, and simultaneously dangerous, lesson of his action: There was no repercussion, no price to pay, no need to tell the truth. There was a lesson for me to learn, as well.

A few days later, I stepped into the *bodega*, innocently happy to see the owner, whom the family had known for some time. As I said hello to him, he asked where Nelson was. Why had he not come into the store in days? He then asked me if Nelson had money. I wasn't yet sure why he was asking me that, so I told him no. The fact was that I didn't see money, I saw toys. He waved his hand to motion me to go behind the counter and pointed to the shelf where he said he had a brown paper bag with dollar bills in it, and that it went missing the last time Nelson worked there. He was sure Nelson had taken it. Only the two of them were ever behind the counter.

Instantly, my logical and analytical young mind went to work, piecing two and two together: the toys, the mysterious mother of a friend, unavailable due to an injury, and then, poof! Vanished!

He then led me to the back room of the *bodega* and showed me a gun. He had me stand beside him as he pulled the trigger twice, piercing a box at the other end of the room. He did not say anything, but I got the message just the same. If anyone stole from him again, they might wind up like that box, with two bullet holes in them. Inside of me, I felt that the lesson I would take away from Nelson's action was that there is always a price to pay for someone's misdeed. That was the very first event in our young lives that I believe set the tone for Nelson's future, and mine.

There was a kid, Henry, who was around our age, hanging out in front of his apartment building across the street from ours. He was this black kid on 179th Street whom we had seen before, but never met or played with. The neighborhood in the early 1960s was predominantly black and Puerto Rican. Nelson and I were walking outside in the summer with nothing to do. We went up to Henry and were hanging around the front of his building when we began play wrestling. It got out of hand and he got upset and decided to go upstairs to his apartment. I guess he felt we roughed him up. The next day, he saw us and invited us to his apartment to meet his parents. Nelson and I thought it was a nice gesture and went along, thinking he wanted to make up for the day before and be friends. I was terrified to see that, upon walking into the apartment, on a table on the left side of the foyer was a holster with a gun. I felt a little more at ease that there was a police badge beside it.

Instantly, I knew we were being given a subtle message—the kid's dad was a cop, so it would be best if we didn't bother him. His parents didn't need to say anymore. They were pleasant with us, said hello, and asked us to sit in the living room. We stayed a few minutes only, and then told them we had to go home. They had successfully delivered their message. Nelson and I didn't say anything to one another about the gun, but it definitely left an impression on me. We never played with Henry again. The funny thing is that we saw him a few years later in East Elmhurst, Queens. His family moved a few blocks from where we moved to on Astoria Boulevard. Small world!

Prior to seeing the *bodega* owner shooting a gun into a cardboard box and seeing Henry's dad's gun on the table, the only gun I had ever seen was a toy gun that Mom bought me one Christmas, complete with its own holster. I remember it was a cap gun that came with small red caps to resemble bullets. Nelson and I played cowboy and Indian or street robbers, making a popping sound, like a real gun, when one of us pulled the trigger with the red cap inserted inside the gun's hammer. When we ran out of caps, or "bullets," we didn't play with the gun anymore.

I was excited that Nelson decided to join me and some friends in a game of stickball on Vyse Avenue, right outside our apartment. That was the first time he played the game with me, so it was an opportunity for me to demonstrate to him what a fun game it was. Most of us always played stickball in the middle of the street, using manhole covers as home plate and second base, and parked cars in between as second and third base, using either a car's tire for the base, or chalking a box on the asphalt. I was excited because I loved playing any form of baseball, whether it was the real game or a derivative, like stickball or punch ball. I had this vision that if I could get Nelson to like the sport, we would be able to spend more time playing together. We could go to Yankee Stadium with Dad to watch a game, or he could join me when I went to play baseball with Papo, my early coach, and friends at the nearby West Farms Square baseball field.

Nelson was playing catcher behind home plate when the batter hit a ball that no one was able to catch. As the batter ran around the bases, one of the outfielders caught up to the ball, relaying it to me in the infield, where I was playing. The runner was rounding second base and scurrying toward third when he decided to try to make it a home run. I threw the pinkish Spalding rubber ball to Nelson at home plate. He correctly stood in front of home plate, but should have slid to one side as the big kid came barreling down the street to score. Nelson caught the ball and waited to tag the runner out. He dropped the ball as the kid ran into him, knocking him down. I ran over to him after I saw him hit the ground and his head bounce off the manhole cover. The ominous sound of his head hitting the steel cover and the sight of it bouncing up frightened me. One of the other kids helped me get him to his feet. His eyes were closed and he mumbled, "Mommy, I'm dead, I'm dead, Mommy I'm dead." That scared me even more because I thought he was unconscious, since he would not open his eyes as I walked him to our apartment.

I told Mom what had happened and begged her to take him to the hospital, but she just laid him on her bed. I stayed with him for a while as he lay there and eventually fell asleep, which scared me even more. Again, I begged Mom to take him to the hospital, that he had fallen asleep, which I thought was also an ominous sign considering the way he hit his head. I don't think Mom grasped the seriousness of his head violently hitting the manhole cover. Perhaps she equated that with his head hitting the asphalt, but I was there and knew it was much worse than that. She never took him to the hospital, and I was fearful that he was going to die.

For years after that, I often half-jokingly said that Nelson was the way he was—irresponsible and impulsive—because of the slamming of his head on that manhole cover. Over the years, I feared the accident caused damage to his brain. It was the same side, the right hemisphere, which now suffered a severe stroke some fifty years later. Who's to know if that fall created a lesion small enough to make him seem normal, but that slowly got worse over the years, eventually blocking the normal flow of blood to that right side? I am not a neurosurgeon or a doctor of any kind, but it seems to me to be too coincidental that the stroke was on the same side where Nelson's head hit that manhole cover.

I remember Mom took us shopping with her on Southern Boulevard when she was buying clothes for us or for herself. Sometimes she would take us to the Vivero on 125th Street in the South Bronx to by a fresh chicken or a hen to make a stew for dinner. The Vivero was a smelly place where people bought live animals like chickens, hens, and goats and had them butchered while they waited. I hated the smell when we went in there and was amazed at seeing all the animals packed tightly in crates from floor to ceiling. It seemed inhumane. The floor was always covered in sawdust to keep people from slipping on wet spots. It was a busy place, as it was customary for people in the Bronx to get their fresh meat there. Mom selected the bird she wanted and a man opened a crate and grabbed it by the neck. I remember thinking how brave he was to go in there to pull out an animal with his bare hands. I thought that he might be bitten, but it seemed that he never was. We plainly saw and heard when the bird stopped clucking after the man snapped its neck. He then quickly removed all its feathers by using a machine to burn and pluck them. The air had a strong, sour smell of live animals mixed with burnt feathers. All this happened in a matter of a few minutes. He then took the bird in the back, where I could hear the sound of a heavy knife or ax as the bird was cut into parts and wrapped in paper, placed in a bag, and handed to Mom, with a separate small brown paper wrapping the gizzards. It was amazing to witness the entire process take place in such a short period of time.

When I was ten years old, Mom sent me on an errand to buy a hen at the same Vivero. She was busy at home and could not go, so she sent me. I was accustomed, by then, to riding the subway by myself, so I thought nothing of it. I got on the train on Tremont Avenue and proceeded to Prospect Avenue, where I got off to go to the Vivero. I knew the routine once I got there; having been with Mom the many times she did it. I walked in and asked one of the workers behind the counter for the hen. I didn't bother picking the one I wanted, because they all looked the same to me. I let the man pick it, kill it, pluck it, then have it cut and bagged for me. Once again, it all happened in a few minutes. I left and headed back to the subway to take the hen home to Mom. I boarded the train and stood by the door, not paying much attention to the stops because I had about four of them before arriving at my Tremont Avenue station.

Suddenly, I saw the darkness of a tunnel as we approached the next station. Immediately, I knew something was wrong. I felt confused and in a twilight zone moment. Why was there a tunnel? All my stops were outdoors. My routine was supposed to be so simple.

I had boarded the train on the wrong side of the platform and headed downtown, instead of uptown. With the bird tucked under my arm, I exited the train at the next stop. I was in a panic and began to cry. I had no idea how to navigate the complexity of switching trains in order to get back home. For that instant, I felt I was lost forever, and would never get back home. I missed Mom, Nelson, Dad, Chubby, Tata, and Susan. Would I ever see them again?

I saw a police officer nearby and ran to him for help. I explained that I was lost. I had to get to Tremont Avenue. Without hesitating to ask me why I was traveling the train alone, he walked me to the platform where I could make my U-turn connection. Once I saw daylight again and the familiarity of the stations I knew—Prospect, Freeman—I relaxed. I made it home! I never told Mom or anyone that I got lost, but always wondered why she didn't send Nelson instead of me on that errand. He was the oldest and more experienced with the streets than I was.

CHAPTER FIVE

On To Queens

The year we moved to East Elmhurst in Queens, New York, Nelson was about to turn fourteen and I was turning twelve. It was at this time that our lives began to go in different directions, even though we continued to do things together. We shared a brotherly closeness that would not yet be broken, even as we developed different interests. I was getting more involved in sports and school; he was exploring working and girls.

Neither of us had much guidance from Mom and Dad, but we responded to that lacking very differently. As I imagine most siblings close in age are, Nelson and I were developing a competitiveness that, at times, felt like jealousy that aroused a sense of inspiration. While I was out playing softball and basketball at twelve years old, Nelson picked up a paper route. He had a green bicycle with long handlebars and a banana seat—courtesy of the "friend's mother" in the Bronx—and used it to deliver newspapers on his route. I remember he had a pocket-sized notebook assigned to him by his boss. In it, he wrote the names and addresses of the homes he delivered newspapers to and how much he had to collect from them each Thursday. I was a bit in awe of my brother, thinking that he had an official job, and not just sweeping floors at the *bodega*. That started me thinking that if Nelson could find a job, I could do the same. Money was always scarce at home, so if I could work, I could have more freedom to buy things I wanted. Nelson didn't know it, but he was my role model at that stage.

It was perplexing to see the newspaper route job falling apart for Nelson. After just a few short weeks, he came home complaining to Mom that his boss was mistreating him and he didn't want to go back there anymore. Mom's advice was that if his boss was not treating him well, he should not go back. She did not inquire further, and did not go to the storefront business on 83rd Street in Jackson Heights to investigate. That was where the newspapers were stored and handed to the delivery boys, and where the delivery boys, like Nelson, had to hand in the fees they collected from customers each week. Being the curious and protective brother that I was, I decided to walk by the business to understand what was going on and why someone was mistreating Nelson. I was surprised to learn from the boss that Nelson had not handed in the fees he collected the prior two weeks. That was the cause of the tension between them. The guy wanted his money, and when he saw he wasn't going to get it, he cut his losses and fired Nelson.

Nelson was pleased because, in his impulsive and shortsighted way of thinking, he got away with someone else's money. When I returned home, I mentioned what I was told to Mom, but she didn't do anything about it. She didn't question Nelson or speak with his boss to get his side of the story. Nelson, by now, had learned that Mom would believe almost anything he told her. He felt privileged and confident that he could talk his way out of any misdeed. As far as I was concerned, Nelson should have been watched much closely and guided to do the right thing. He was beginning to show signs of a dangerously impulsive pattern of behavior. Mom repeatedly dismissed his transgressions as unimportant and the result of Nelson being unlucky.

CHAPTER SIX

Guayama

In the summer of 1970, Nelson was restless at home and asked Mom to send him to Puerto Rico to stay with her family in Guayama. He had learned that his natural dad, Benjamin, was on the island, and thought it would be a good time to see him, as well. Mom was always open with Puchi about his natural dad, even though they were separated before he was born. Nelson visited his dad on occasion in the South Bronx and developed a relationship with his stepbrothers and stepsisters. I met Benjamin only once and could see that Nelson inherited some of his physical features. They had the same nose and same hazel-colored eyes. Over the years, I saw that he also inherited the impulsive, personality that Mom often described Benjamin as having.

Nelson was in Puerto Rico for about one month when Dad decided he would take a trip there and invited me to go along. Nelson was staying at Mom's aunt's house, whom we all called Tia Isabella. Dad and I first journeyed to Mayaguez to visit with his parents, Abuela Ernestina and Abuelo Eleodoro. I was excited to go and packed my own suitcase with nice clothes, an extra pair of Converse sneakers, a pair of Playboy shoes to dress up, along with a couple of colorful sweaters I had, which I learned once there I could not wear in the island's sweltering summer heat. I anticipated that Nelson would introduce me to some of the girls in town and I would be a double hit with everyone, as his brother and as a New Yorker.

Dad had arranged through my Uncle Raphael (Papo) to pick us up at the airport in San Juan. Dad would pay the driver twenty-five dollars. After we landed and went outside, I was once again excited to breathe the warm and humid air and to see the palm trees swaying ever so slightly in the Caribbean breeze. It was happily reminiscent of my first trip to the island with Mom and my brothers and sister. The sun was shining, just like the last time when Mom took us there to give birth to Susan. The airport was buzzing with people speaking Spanish and greeting arriving visitors and returning family and friends. I was amazed, just as last time, at how friendly everyone was. I was older now, at thirteen, and much more attuned and interested in how beautiful and voluptuous the girls were. I could not wait to get to Guayama to see and meet the girls there. But first we had to go to Mayaguez, which I was not looking forward to. Somehow, I had a premonition that that leg of our trip to the island was not going to be a happy one.

My eyes and head were turning constantly as we drove from the airport to Mayaguez, and I didn't want to miss a single sight. Everything was much more noticeable to me: the roosters and chickens on the side of the roads, the farmers carrying their fruits and vegetables, or the lone farmer with his machete in hand. That sight made me think that if someone was walking in the Bronx or Queens with a machete, he would quickly be arrested. In Puerto Rico, it was commonplace and generally without a malicious purpose in mind. Occasionally, I would see someone on the side of the road selling quenepas, which I loved to eat and was sure I would have plenty of when we arrived at Abuela's or at Tia Isabella's.

As the ride to Mayaguez was a long two or three hours, midway through, the driver stopped at a roadside restaurant where we were going to have lunch. The place was simple, darkly lit, with a counter and a few tables scattered throughout the room. The food was typical Puerto Rican fare, with rice and beans and an assortment of fried meats. The driver and Dad ordered and we all ate *carnitas fritas*, deep fried, succulent pork pieces, with rice and beans and *plantanos maduros* (the super sweet fried plantains that I loved). They had a beer or two to wash the food down with and I had a can of Cola Champagne, a cola that I loved, but could only find either in Puerto Rico or *bodegas* in the South Bronx. Once we moved to Queens, I could no longer find it. I loved it better than Coca Cola because it had the taste of bubblegum mixed with coke. I considered it Puerto Rican coca cola.

It was a tasty lunch, except that the driver lost a cap after biting into a piece of crunchy fried pork. He put the tooth in his pocket, so he wouldn't completely lose it, and we finished our meal. He and Dad chatted nonstop the entire trip. They never had a minute for me, but I was at peace checking out all the sights as we drove. We finally arrived at Abuela's house at 55 Dulce Palito Street. We got out of the car to get our bags and stretch our legs and walked into the house. We were greeted by Abuela, Abuelo, and my Aunt Jeannette, who still had not married and continued to live with her parents. The house looked exactly the same as the last time I was there some seven years back. The difference this time was that one of my favorite uncles, Edwin, now lived across the street after getting divorced from his wife, Miriam, in New York. I used to visit their house often in the Bronx and was disappointed to hear that they had gotten divorced.

I found that there wasn't very much to do on the block where my grandparents lived, and they were not the most communicative people. I recalled the scratches on my legs from the last trip when I sat on the porch with my legs sticking out of the bottom of the chain-link fence, so I wasn't about to do that again. My legs were bigger now, anyway, and probably would not have fit. I walked over to the house at the end where the large mango tree was just to see if it was still there. It was, but I wasn't as interested as I used to be in stealing the lady's mangoes. I decided to walk downtown and buy a Cola Champagne soda at the *bodega*. It was so hot outside that I drank the entire can while at the store and bought another one. In one afternoon, I must have gone back to that store three times for Cola Champagne. The streets were pretty quiet, so I became bored rather quickly. It seemed like Nelson and Guayama were so close and we could not get there fast enough.

That first evening at Abuela's, Dad went to Edwin's house across the street and left me in her care. I was going crazy! All they did was sit around the living room without a word being spoken. Abuela sat in her cane-backed mahogany rocking chair, Abuelo was in his matching one, and Jeannette in another. They didn't ask me about school, my friends, or anything else, for that matter. I sat near them on a dining room chair, bored out of my mind. As night fell around us, Dad was still not home. I stepped out on the porch and could hear him in the house across the street. I could tell from the loud conversation and the clanking of the dominoes that they were having a fun time playing and drinking, probably rum and coke. I didn't like when Dad drank because he got sick and said silly things. He usually threw up every time he drank too much, and picked a fight with Mom. At home, at least we had Mom to shelter us from his drunken malaise and our room to hide in. At Abuela's house, I didn't know what to expect, as I didn't have a place to hide.

It was 10 p.m. when he finally stumbled into the house. The front door was still open, as it usually was all day long and until it was time to go to bed. Dad grabbed for something, anything, with one arm as he tried to balance his wobbly body. He found a place to sit, and then all hell broke loose. I was already bored and sad because there was nothing to do that evening while he was across the street getting drunk. I was also anxious to get to Guayama and hang out with Nelson. I thought that was the entire purpose of our trip and was somewhat disappointed that we had to go to Mayaguez first. On top of that, the sight of Dad drunk and hardly able to walk frightened me. It felt like an overwhelming of melancholy and I just burst into tears. I didn't know how to tell my dad that I didn't want to be there, that I wanted to be in Guayama with Nelson. I didn't want to see him drunk and out of control. It made him look weak and fragile, and I detested that. I wanted a dad who was in control, strong, and purposeful.

All of a sudden, he started crying and mumbling. He scolded Abuela in his incoherent speech. I had to stop crying and pay close attention to him to understand what he was saying. He recalled the story Mom had told him years earlier when we returned home unexpectedly from Abuela's house the time that Susan was going to be born. He told Abuela that she had treated Mom badly. He was hurt by it and would never forgive her for that. Abuela was nonchalant about it and dismissive. She didn't engage him in the argument, recognizing that he was drunk and not in control of all his faculties. I couldn't believe that he was bringing that up! It had nothing to do with the present day or circumstances. He could have easily called her the day after Mom returned home to ask Abuela what happened. If not then, he could have asked her in the afternoon when we first arrived and gotten it out of the way. It seemed odd to me that he would bring it up now that he was drunk. I suppose that in a drunken stupor, it was easier for him to work up the courage to confront his mom.

Now that I was thirteen, I had witnessed enough of my parents' behavior that I suspected Mom overreacted to the argument with Abuela and used it as an excuse to go back home, surprising Dad in case he was doing something he should not have been doing. He should have known this about her as well and let the issue ride with Abuela. The way she dismissed his behavior that night, it felt like she was thinking that "These people are nuts!" I can't remember if it was part of the plan or another sudden exit, but the next morning we had coffee and bread and left to head southeast to Guayama. The same driver who picked us up at the airport took us to Guayama. I was kind of sad to leave Abuela's house. I felt guilty about the night before. I didn't think she or my grandfather deserved the outburst and disruption in their usual calm lives.

It seemed like it was another long, three-hour drive through the back roads and rural towns between the two locations. I was so anxious to get to see Nelson that I don't even remember if we stopped along the way for something to eat. When we got into town and pulled up beside Tia Isabella's house, it was like a scene in the *Godfather Part II* when a young Don Corleone, portrayed by Robert De Niro, returns home to Corleone, Italy, with his wife and children. When their car arrives at the family home, they are enthusiastically greeted by a waiting crowd of family and friends. This time it was Dad and me getting out of the car and people from the neighborhood coming out and swarming us like we were some sort of celebrities: the wealthy New Yorkers had arrived. They had no idea that we were poor people living in Queens with five children sharing one bedroom. They simply imagined that if we lived in New York, we must be special. Nelson had helped by talking about us in such a way that raised expectations of our arrival. He was like our agent with the townspeople. Of course, he was right there waiting for us. We hugged and he proudly led us inside Tia Isabella's small house and showed me where to put my things. I hastily unpacked my suitcase on top of the bed we would share so we could go outside. He wanted to introduce me to friends, cousins, and other relatives. I didn't know any of them and had only heard Mom talking about Tia Isabella, my maternal grandfather's sister, and Mama Juana, my maternal great-grandmother.

Tia Isabella was Mom's aunt, and the only sibling that Abuelo Julio had. She was his older sister by seven years. Tia Isabella was black like Abuelo and just as sweet as he was. She hugged and kissed me when we first arrived, and was kind to Dad, as well. It was my very first time in Guayama, and so the first time I was meeting my mom's side of the family there. I was amazed and proud that I was meeting a relative of Mom's that was born in 1904, as Tia Isabella was. Nelson took me around the two or three blocks where everyone he knew lived and introduced me to people whom I can't remember if they were just friends or relatives. We walked to the center of town in the middle of the afternoon and bought delicious pineapple ices. Even though they were fruit and water, somehow they tasted creamy. They were much better than the ices we got in stores back in New York, and freshly made that same morning. One of the highlights of my visit to Guayama was when Nelson took me to meet Mama Juana. She lived by herself in a one-room house around the corner from her daughter, Tia Isabella. Nelson was like the mayor of the town, saying hello to everyone as we walked the streets, and everyone greeting him in return. I was proud to be with my brother.

We called Mama Juana 'Abuelita' out of respect. We walked into her house and Nelson introduced me as his brother, son of Julia, the name the family called Mom. Abuelita was ninety-five years old at the time I first met her. She had a thin, short unlit cigar in her mouth, which shocked me. I had never seen a lady with a cigar. How could a lady so old be smoking a cigar? I thought only men smoked them. As I got close when she asked me to approach her for a hug and a kiss, I was taken aback by how wrinkled her skin was and how much the bottom of her raised right arm sagged and swayed in the air. She had a band on her hair to keep it out of her face in the heat. I was amazed to meet a family relative who was born way back in 1875. It was an absolute honor to meet her. How many people get to meet a great-grandparent that was ninety-five years old? She was beautifully happy, smiling and peaceful in her own home. She blessed us and we each hugged her one more time before we left. I always wondered who my great-grandfather was, because Abuelita was white, but Abuelo and Tia Isabella were black. I imagined that he must have been black and come from Africa. They were definitely not descendants of the native Taíno Indians, whose skin tone was more olive than black. I asked my grandfather, Julio, about his father, and was saddened to hear that he never met him. I thought to myself, "Here is a man I have known all my life as one of the happiest people I knew, always smiling, hugging, kissing, just like his mom, yet he never knew his dad." How sad!

That evening, Nelson and I were to sleep in a small bedroom in Tia Isabella's house. I was a New Yorker accustomed to a much different lifestyle than the people in this rural Puerto Rican town had, and so many things were new and surprising to me. As Nelson and I got into bed, I noticed that above us was an opening in the roof of the one-story house. It was covered with wire mesh, but I wasn't too sure that critters were not able to get into the room. I asked Nelson why there was an opening.

"It's to let air in because it gets too hot," he told me.

Once I got over the fear of the possibility of animals getting in—like bats, rats, or lizards—I enjoyed gazing at the night sky and the stars from the bed. Then I saw a lizard sitting on the wire screen. No sooner did I relax when Nelson scared me right out of the covers. He brushed my feet with his foot and made a sound as if the lizard had gotten in. I jumped out of the bed. That was Nelson, always pulling some kind of prank to scare me and get a laugh out of it.

Tia Isabella's son, Raul Ortiz, lived around the corner from her house in the opposite direction from Abuelita. The next day we went to visit with his family. They were preparing food for a dinner. On the porch, they had baskets of potatoes that they were peeling and placing in buckets. I guessed they were going to cook them later, perhaps to make *papas rellenas*, stuffed potato balls made from mashed potatoes stuffed with a meat stew, dredged in flour, then deep fried. Delicious! Somehow, I was roped into peeling potatoes on the porch. I was not happy about it, but the people were so nice, I didn't refuse. I didn't want word getting back to Tia Isabella, or Mom, that I was not helpful. Nelson left me there and I spent the entire afternoon peeling and grating what I thought were hundreds of potatoes. I had never peeled or grated potatoes before, and wound up scraping my knuckles against the grater. It was one of those standing, four-sided graters they wanted me to lean into the bowl so that the potato collected in it. For the rest of our trip, I avoided going to that block at all cost.

Dad had fun there, as well. In the evening, he hung out at a neighbor's house with Raul and got drunk while they played dominoes. It was very different than in Mayaguez, though. I hung out with Nelson and all the kids that lived nearby, so I wasn't bored. I didn't even notice when Dad returned at night to Tia's house. Our visit there lasted five days, until we had to return to New York. It was sad to leave because Nelson stayed to spend the entire summer there.

When the summer was over, Nelson returned home to New York to get ready for school. He was entering the eighth grade at IS 145 in Jackson Heights and I was entering the seventh at the same school. I was transferring from P.S. 127 in East Elmhurst and excited that I would be reunited with him at the same school.

CHAPTER SEVEN

The Showman

By now, I was sensing more clearly that Nelson had a penchant for attention and wanted to stand out in a crowd. I thought that was a good trait in him that would bring him great success—if properly channeled. Sometimes we both pursued the same things, but for different reasons and with different outcomes in mind.

At school, he saw an opportunity to become chief of the crossing guards and went for it. He was particularly attracted to the hardware that came with the role. He wanted to wear, in public, the white plastic belt that wrapped over his shoulder and around his waist. The big item, though, was the shiny silver badge with the center seal painted a bright red that said "Captain." Nelson wore it proudly for everyone to see around the school, and outside as well. He wanted me to get involved and become part of the organization. He convinced me to join, and appointed me as his lieutenant. It was somewhat of a family-run operation. He held a ceremony in the auditorium with about six of his guards and announced my appointment, handing me the belt and a badge, which had a bright blue seal. My job was to supervise the guards and help protect kids from vehicles at the intersection of Northern Boulevard across 79th and 80th Streets.

Unfortunately, he had a short attention span for that role and the responsibility it brought. I was stunned and surprised when, only a few weeks after getting the job, he quit. He simply quit! I was so excited to be working with my brother that his voluntary departure confused and saddened me. I was looking forward to building something with him. It was an opportunity for us to be close in sharing a common cause. It turned out to be a bit of wishful thinking on my part!

As time went on, I realized that his motivation for acquiring the post was purely for the novelty of wearing the badge and belt. He felt good to be seen wearing it, but didn't care for the responsibility it brought. It was actually work, and he didn't care for that. His modus operandi was that once the novelty wore off, he quickly abandoned the role and sought something else. I was too young to recognize that what he needed was someone to watch over him and guide him. With each demonstration of his impulsiveness, we grew farther apart.

I, on the other hand, felt obligated to carry out the duties of the role. I embraced the responsibility with a determination that was, perhaps, the other extreme to Nelson's. When he vacated the captain's post, the other guards voted to elect me to that role. I felt surprised by the support they gave me and was honored to lead them. The commitment with which I executed the responsibilities of that role came at a cost. I remember meeting with my guards each morning around 7 a.m. as we prepared to take our posts before students began arriving. I instructed them to make sure they did not allow anyone to jaywalk around the four corners of the school we guarded. One morning, one of my guards came back with a bloody nose and crying. He tried to stop a kid from jaywalking and was punched in the face. I realized that although we were trying to do the right thing, not everyone appreciated it.

Mini-bikes were suddenly popular in the early seventies. One kid in the neighborhood, a few blocks from our apartment and near our grandparents' home, had one. It was a bright metallic blue Honda bike with a headlight, as fancy as a larger road motorcycle. The kid drove it up and down the block, and enjoyed showing it off. I fantasized driving it, but that was about the extent of my admiration. I didn't think about getting one because I knew we could not afford it. For Nelson, it was the subject of his next conquest. I don't know how he did it, but he convinced Mom to buy him one. It was an extravagant purchase for a poor family. Dad's annual income could not have been more than five or six thousand dollars a year, and that had to suffice for seven of us.

Nelson and Mom took the Long Island Railroad all the way out to Port Jefferson to pick up the red mini-bike he wanted. Somehow, they brought it back the same way. Nelson drove it on the sidewalk on Astoria Boulevard or on 94th Street, where he could take it the two blocks up to my grandparents' neighborhood and ride with the kid who had the blue one. I begged him to let me drive it, but he always said no. The more I begged him, the more he refused me. I even asked the other kid to let me drive his blue one, but he refused as well.

Finally, one sunny afternoon, Nelson decided to let me drive it. I remember we were in the middle of 94th Street and 31st Avenue around the corner from Abuela's house. The kid with the blue Honda and Nelson were driving up and down the street.

"Nelson, let me drive it."

"Okay, here, you can drive it."

I was so excited! I had no idea how to drive it, and he didn't show me. He must have felt that since I knew how to ride a bicycle, I would know how to ride the mini-bike. There were some differences, though. I didn't know that the motor below the seat got so hot that it would burn you badly if you touched it. With no warning whatsoever, I approached the mini-bike to sit on it. As I leaned it toward me to raise my right leg over the seat and climb on it, my left leg touched the scorching hot motor and burned me. I still drove the bike down the street and back, but it wasn't as much fun as I had envisioned. In retrospect, the reason Nelson let me drive it was that he was tiring of the novelty of the mini-bike. He hardly drove it much after that. It was time for him to move on to something else.

Nelson always looked for something to do that had him stand out in a crowd. Partly because our uncle, Ivan, was into practicing martial arts, and partly because he was watching Bruce Lee movies, Nelson's next escapade was to portray himself as a martial arts expert. I remember he somehow got his hands on a karate suit and wore it outside for all the kids in the neighborhood to see. He would make basic moves—accentuated with grunts— to give any ignorant spectator the impression that he knew what he was doing. I could never tell if he was as much influenced by Ivan as by Bruce Lee. It was most assuredly a little of both. I would have had to get into his head to find out, because he was not going to tell me. He wanted to give the impression that it all came to him naturally.

The fact was that he saw Ivan one afternoon come out from Abuela's house wearing his karate suit to break up a fight that he and I were in. The Haitian family that lived on the first floor where my grandparents first moved to in Queens included two brothers, Karl and Jean. Karl was a nice kid, taller than his brother and more athletic. Jean fancied himself a good athlete, but was actually clumsy and with poor coordination. He also had a grotesque lump on the front of his right foot whose protrusion could always be seen in his sneaker. It made him walk with a limp. That was probably a source of his lack of coordination. I often played baseball, basketball, or football with them. Nelson, who, as I've said, was not interested in sports, knew them from hanging out on the streets of East Elmhurst.

One afternoon, as we were playing outside on 92nd Street and 31st Avenue, Nelson got into an argument with Jean, who had a big mouth and could easily make himself an irritant. Of course, Nelson was not one to back down, even if he got the worst of an encounter. The verbal altercation became a physical one. Nelson and Jean got into a shoving match when Karl went over, probably to break it up, and Nelson swung at him. At that point, Karl wound up on top of Nelson on the ground. Jean, the coward that he was, got into the fray. Then I jumped on top of Jean, punching him in his back as hard as I could.

That's when someone got word to someone at Abuela's house that we were fighting outside. Ivan, who was also a track star at Newtown High School, came downstairs in his karate suit and pulled everyone apart. Fight over! Jean was the only one crying, thinking that Ivan, the respected martial arts expert and track star, punched him in the back. I told him that it was me who punched him, not Ivan. He kept saying that it couldn't have been me: "He hit me too hard. It couldn't have been you." Proud that he thought he got hit pretty hard—by me, I smirked and walked away. Nelson saw Ivan's domination over that fracas, and decided, along with what he saw in Bruce Lee's movies, that he had to be a martial arts expert. He imagined that he would be feared and respected as Ivan was.

I wish that I had been old enough back then to see what, ironically, only a lifetime of experiences has opened my eyes to. Nelson was a showman. He was like Liberace, the flamboyant Las Vegas entertainer, or more like a cross between him and Hector "Macho" Camacho, the Puerto Rican Junior lightweight boxer who often entered the ring wearing eye-catching costumes. He just needed someone to help him channel that charisma, that desire to entertain a crowd.

He wore his karate suit around the neighborhood and walked with the confidence of a hero. He never, ever, took one single lesson in karate, or any other martial art, for that matter. He didn't read books to learn about the arts, either. He just wanted to play the part of a martial arts expert, but not become one. Faking it, whatever *it* is, usually spawns unintended consequences. That was something Nelson could not imagine. Suddenly, younger kids in the neighborhood saw him walking around with his karate suit and a pair of nunchucks. Impressionable as kids are, they approached him to ask about his skills. They wanted to know if he could teach them the martial art of karate. Well, Nelson's eyes lit up. He had unintentionally stumbled upon a business opportunity. It became a chain reaction of unintended, unexpected consequences. He began taking money for lessons from the kids, who might have ranged in age from ten to twelve. Nelson was fifteen at that point.

The problem was that he could not teach them what he did not know. The basic karate punch and the inexpert side kick could not fill the lessons he promised them for the buck or two in fees paid. The kids grew disenchanted pretty quickly. Soon, parents and older brothers came by and requested refunds. Nelson's impulsiveness got him into trouble again. If he could have only thought things through—weighed pros and cons, cause and effect, actions and possible reactions—he could have done the right thing and avoided controversy. That was not his nature, however. Unfortunately, Mom and Dad were too aloof to recognize that he had a talent that begged to be developed, and some brewing deficiencies that required serious discipline.

My brother Nelson was indeed talented. A few years later, I saw him pick up a trombone after being mesmerized at witnessing Willie Colon, the Salsa musician, play his. Where did he get these things from? Here we were a poor family and whatever he wanted, he got. The basic theme remained the same. He saw how the crowd adored and applauded Willie Colon's trombone playing, and instantly, the inspiration entered his body like an electric charge that powered him to respond. His usual resourcefulness landed him a trombone that he practiced in preparation for his next adventure. I never knew where he got it from. And he only had it until the novelty, once again, wore off. But this time this next exploit was a real stepping-stone. He had a musical inclination that he had inherited from Mom's side of the family.

Abuelo Julio was both an electrician and a musician in Guayama, Puerto Rico, in the 1930s and part of the 1940s, before he made his way to New York City in 1946 at the age of thirty-five. In fact, in one U.S. census survey, he was listed as a musician. He was the source of live music at homes throughout the small town of Guayama. He was sought after to play his accordion with his group of musicians at house parties and events at the Plaza de Guayama. When he arrived in New York on August 28, 1946, with his brother-in-law, Flor Soto, to live on Beck Street in the South Bronx, the next day he went out to buy a new accordion. His music was a high priority.

Nelson's penchant for music, which was beginning to sprout, had very good roots in Abuelo. Both were self-taught and good at that particular art. No one paid too much attention to what Nelson was doing with his trombone in those early days. Mom and Dad did not do anything to either encourage or guide him. But by the time he was eighteen or nineteen, he discovered his natural calling. I was stunned when, one evening, I saw him on stage. I had heard he was going to play at a small club on 37th Avenue in Corona, Queens, so I went to see him. I was eager to lend my support and help fill the venue. He had plenty of friends in the area that crowded the site, along with regulars who hadn't yet heard of Nelson Marrero. He was so enchanted that he didn't even notice I was there. But I was astounded in what I saw! He stood on the stage and played the trombone and sang a Salsa song as if he had been trained at the Julliard School. He took command of that stage with a passion and the raw talent that he finally discovered all by himself.

Before he settled on music, Nelson dabbled in almost anything that would muster attention from an audience. We had several uncles who were regular fans of Pro Wrestling's Lucha Libre in the early 1970s. They frequently went to Madison Square Garden to the Saturday night matches. Sometimes they invited Nelson and me to go with them. We enjoyed watching from the rafters of MSG. That was during the era of wrestlers like Pedro Morales, who was champion for a time and a favorite of ours because he was Puerto Rican. There was also Bruno Sammartino, George Steele, Gorilla Monsoon, and, Nelson's absolute idol, Chief Jay Strongbow, who portrayed a Native American wrestler.

After a few Saturday nights at Madison Square Garden watching the way Chief Jay Strongbow pranced around the ring, Nelson became enchanted with his style. The wrestler entered the ring with a traditional American Indian colorful feathered headdress and went on the "warpath" when the fans started cheering him against an opponent. The fans went absolutely berserk as the Chief danced around his weakened opponent, hitting him in the head with his hip or his signature tomahawk chop until the opponent could no longer stand and the Chief won. Of all his signature moves, from the ones just mentioned to the sleeper hold and the Indian death lock, Nelson loved the hip kick. He was also mesmerized with the manner in which the fans loved Chief Jay Strongbow when he danced with his feathered headdress on before the start of a match.

He wanted to imitate the Chief, and to do so, he began to wrestle with a small group of friends. He easily convinced them to join him in his new adventure. They had to be younger than he was to assure that he could manage to dominate them in the ring with the Chief's war dance and his hip kick. I remember that we went to the Lost Battalion sports center on Queens Boulevard for our impromptu wrestling matches. I used to go there to play basketball, and one day noticed that, in a lower level of the facility, they had a boxing ring. Once I mentioned that to Nelson, it gave him the missing piece to his newly discovered enterprise. He gathered up the members of his wrestling group and they marched to the Lost Battalion. There he could dance around the ring, make his Indian howls as he circled his smaller opponent and lowered his head so he could reach it with his hip kick. The kick wasn't hard—he wasn't trying to hurt him. It was more of a demonstration of his masterful imitation of his wrestling idol.

***

It's been nearly three months since he suffered the stroke. Nelson has been shuttled between two hospitals in Connecticut and a nursing home, where he receives physical therapy. His condition really hasn't improved, though the family has occasionally sensed glimmers of hope that he will come back to us. Susan continues to visit him on a weekly basis and is closest to witness his current condition. She mentions to me that he has opened his eyes, but seems to stare into space. I can tell that she felt a sense of relief when she told me he had opened his eyes; it implies improvement.

It is confusing to know if he is able to see her: his eyes appear to follow her as she moves around the room. Yet, he does not look straight at her. She asks him if he knows who she is, and he nods his head ever so slightly to indicate that he does. She squeezes his hand and asks him to squeeze hers if he feels her, which he does. Sometimes he moves his right arm halfway up and down, but not his left side. It all gives us hope that he may pull completely out of his vegetative state and that he can safely be removed from life support. Then, he develops a series of infections that require him to be shuttled back to the hospital. He undergoes treatment for the infections, more CT scans, and further observation. Another setback! He becomes unresponsive again.

My other sister, Evelyn, begins to get involved after herself recovering from debilitating back surgery. While the rest of the siblings support giving Nelson time to improve, Evelyn does not. She believes that he will not recover and wants him removed from life support. She lobbies Maritza, the only one with the authority to do so, to elect to have the respirator removed. Even though the doctors continue to inform us that he is not brain dead, she repeatedly tells each of us, separately, in phone calls and text messages, that Nelson is brain dead and not coming back. It is gut-wrenchingly difficult for the entire family. We all want Nelson to get better, but how long do we wait? Had he been removed from life support earlier when the doctors told us he had only a ten percent chance of improving, we wouldn't have seen him open his eyes, or move his right arm. The ordeal has been complicated by the fact that Nelson does not have a Living Will or a

Health Care Proxy to appoint someone to speak for him when he cannot.

So we hang on a while longer with the little hope that remains.

CHAPTER EIGHT
Fractured Brotherhood

When I was fourteen, I began dating my first girlfriend, Cynthia Lester. She lived near us in East Elmhurst. I met her one afternoon as I passed her house on Curtis Street on my way to Vivian's house, the girl whom I wanted to date. Vivian was ambivalent about dating me, though she wouldn't come out and just say so. On my way to her house, Cynthia, who I did not know at that point, was looking out the window of her one-story ranch home. She waved at me as I walked in front of her house. It was sheer coincidence that I walked on Curtis Street. She must have guessed and hoped that I would walk there as well; I could have taken any number of other routes to Vivian's place. Cynthia opened the front door and came outside to introduce herself. She was pretty and quite charming. She mentioned to me that she knew Vivian and wanted to talk to me. She knew I was going over to her house, but she would talk me out of that. Apparently, Vivian, according to Cynthia, was not interested in going out with me and asked Cynthia to intercede. I wound up not going. Instead, I stayed on Cynthia's steps and we talked for a while. Almost immediately, we began dating.

Once Cynthia was comfortable in our relationship, she confessed: Vivian wanted to go out with me, but Cynthia talked her out of it, suggesting we were not right for each other. I was fourteen and Vivian was thirteen. We were naïve and no match for the sixteen-year-old Cynthia. Evidently, Cynthia had seen me walking by on previous occasions and decided she wanted to go out with me. I also learned that before she met me she was interested in Nelson, but he was not interested in her.

I was already uncomfortable with what I felt were Cynthia's devious tactics, so when Nelson told me he had a girlfriend, Cookie, who had a friend he thought I should meet, I took the train ride with him to the Bronx to meet her. Cynthia and I had been dating for a couple of months at that point. Nelson and I went up to Allerton Avenue on the New Lots Number 2 train from 42nd Street, after connecting there from the Flushing Number 7 train and the Times Square shuttle. Nelson's girlfriend, Cookie, an Italian-American girl, introduced me to Robin Wolfson, a Jewish girl. As we walked along Allerton Avenue, I noticed from the corner of my eye that Robin nodded up and down to Cookie. Knowing that I had been approved, I could relax and be myself, I thought. Cookie lived with her mom in a house a couple of blocks away. Her mom was working, so she invited us all to her home where we could spend the afternoon, making sure to leave before her mom was scheduled to return.

I had already decided not to date Cynthia any longer and focus on my relationship with Robin, whom I liked very much. I had not gone over to visit Cynthia to break the news to her, but as far as I was concerned, we were done. I felt completely betrayed when Robin confronted me to tell me that she heard that I had another girlfriend. At first, I was stunned and didn't know what she was talking about. Besides, with her living in the Bronx and me in Queens, we knew none of the same people for her to know anything about me unless I told her. That's when she informed me that Nelson had told her I had a girlfriend named Cynthia. I think I convinced Robin that I stopped seeing Cynthia the day she and I began dating. That evening, I called Cynthia and told her we needed to talk. I went over to her house, sat at the kitchen table with her, and broke the news to her: We could no longer go out together. She seemed sad, although I could never tell if her feelings were genuine or just theatrics, and she returned a ring of mine she was holding on to.

The more damaging part of that experience was what Nelson had done to me. He betrayed my trust! I could not understand why he did that. It was almost as if he saw that I was happy and he didn't like it. He didn't ask me what my intentions were with Cynthia. He didn't ask me if I was still seeing her. He knew that I wasn't going over there because during all my time after school and working, I was in the Bronx with Robin. Most times, he and I went up there together. That is, until he got tired of seeing Cookie. I had a growing sense that, while I was more of a long-term thinker, Nelson was a shortsighted one. I wanted to focus on my relationship with Robin to make it a lasting one. Nelson did not think that way. I enjoyed taking the train with him to the Bronx and hanging out with him up there with Cookie and Robin, but I wondered how long it would last before he would stop seeing her. I knew I would be disappointed when the day came, just like I was when he quit the safety squad at IS 145.

One evening, the four of us were walking along Allerton Avenue on our way to the Bronx Park. It had been raining earlier and Nelson was holding an umbrella. He got into an argument with Cookie, and Robin and I were bystanders to the confrontation. He decided that he wanted to frighten Cookie. In retrospect, he was developing his exit plan. He whispered to me, "Watch this." And he yelled at Cookie and slammed the umbrella several times against the side of a brick building until it broke. It was a show he put on to frighten her away. It was better if she decided that she no longer wanted to see him than for him to break the news to her. Either way, he had enough of the relationship. He wasn't going to return to the Bronx to see her anymore. They spoke on the phone on a few occasions, but it was over. It was sad for me because I enjoyed sharing the experience of hanging out with Nelson. We were brothers growing up together. I felt that it was wonderful for us as brothers to be close. We talked as we rode the train, or walked the streets, and protected each other. It was a much different feeling than being with a friend. We slept in the same room at home and could extend our days together into the night, recalling events of the day and sharing stories about our girlfriends. We could make plans for the next day or the next time we would go to the Bronx together. It was special to me, but, like the IS 145 safety squad, it did not last. Nelson was so engulfed in his impulsiveness that it didn't occur to him that his actions were negatively affecting us as brothers. It was the way our parents taught us to be and he embraced it, while I shunned it.

Soon he began working at McDonald's on Astoria Boulevard and 88th Street. It didn't occur to me at the time that it was common for a sixteen-year-old to work at the best known burger place. I was just proud that my brother worked there and that I could go into the restaurant and be served by him. Every now and then, I went in to buy a burger, fries, and a small Coke. Back then, one could do that with a dollar and get change back. Nelson enjoyed being generous, even with other people's possessions. He would throw in a few extra burgers and bags of fries. No one at the restaurant ever noticed, and he got away with it. It was unfortunate that Mom and Dad did not reprimand him for that. Even though we were kids, Nelson was doing things that were not proper and felt no ramifications for his actions. Mom and Dad knew he was stealing from McDonald's and did not say anything about it. They benefitted from his improper generosity by eating the burgers and fries. By this time, at sixteen years old, Nelson had amassed a pile of actions that required discipline for his sake, but that he never received. Mom and Dad's own weaknesses and ambivalence fed and encouraged Nelson's negative behavior. It impacted him greatly in his future. At the time, I knew that his actions were wrong, and wondered why they did nothing about it. I thought that Mom favored him so much that she could not fault him, but that was just part of the reason. The other was that she did not know how to discipline any of us in a constructive way to shape us into good, productive human beings. Nelson was talented, but also weak. He did not have the strength of character to find guidance outside our home.

During his sophomore year at Newtown High School, Nelson dropped out. He told Mom that he no longer wanted to go to school. She went to the school with him to sign him out. His school days were over. I was a freshman that year and, once again, lost my brother. I was looking forward to the experience of going to school together, but that would not last. High school was somewhat of a family affair. My Uncle Ivan was a senior and my Aunt Millie was a sophomore when I was a freshman. We protected each other whenever issues came up. During his freshman year, Nelson had gotten beat up by a bunch of kids. Millie told me who did it. In those days, I never backed down from a fight, and told her we would take care of it when I joined the school the following year.

Despite the cracks beginning to show in our relationship as brothers, I still protected Nelson. I saw him as vulnerable, and felt a need to look after him. One day as we were between classes, Millie and I saw the kids who beat up Nelson. We confronted them in the staircase, and a fight ensued. It was like a fight scene out of a movie, with a crowd of spectators hollering as the bell for the next class rang in the background. We got the better of the kids and settled the score. But we were late for class. Feeling that we vindicated the family, Millie and I went our separate ways to class. Flustered and sweaty, I hurried to my seat, knowing I was likely to be reprimanded for being late.

No sooner had I sat in my chair when I heard my name called over the PA system. I was immediately summoned to the dean's office. With oohs and aahs from the rest of the class, I rose from my chair and went to the dean's office. When I saw Millie sitting in the office, I knew we were in trouble. Someone had sold us out! The dean was livid. He considered me the instigator of the fight. Placing his right hand on his left arm along the top of his bicep, he threatened to suspend me from school.

"If you ever do something like that again, or get into another fight, I will write a report on you this long and suspend you."

I promised not to do that again. He didn't yell at Millie. That was the end of our meeting. He didn't reprimand us beyond the threat of suspension for me. We were allowed to return to class.

After dropping out of school and quitting the job at McDonald's, Nelson got a job at Jack in the Box across the street from his former employer. Since he didn't have a school schedule, he worked during the day. Nelson invited me to get a job there when he learned there was an opening. I was only fifteen years old, and there were some legal restrictions as to the number of hours I could work during school days. On Nelson's recommendation, the management hired me to work four hours per day after school. As it turned out, Nelson and I never worked the same shift together. He worked the morning shift, which ended when mine started at 6 p.m. It was probably a good thing that we didn't work at the same time. I was a perfectionist and determined to do things by the book. He was cavalier and quick to cut corners. We definitely would have clashed. Nonetheless, I was grateful that he got me the job there. He appeared to be proud as well that I was working there, thanks to him.

I ended up working for the company for three years. Nelson quit a short while after I started. But before he quit, we shared in the experience of an ugly fight. Nelson came by the restaurant to visit while I was working one evening. He was confronted inside the restaurant by the brother of a kid who had paid Nelson for karate lessons. The guy was much bigger than Nelson and wanted the money back. When Nelson refused, the guy grabbed him and lifted him by the neck as he pressed him against the glass wall at the front of the restaurant. I was stunned as I stood behind the counter. I was going outside to intercede when the guy let Nelson go. Nelson then came into the back of the restaurant and grabbed a pot. He filled it with hot grease from the bin we used to fry French fries in. He ran to the other side with the pot and threw its contents at the guy. I thought that if he burned the guy's face and body, he was about to get into serious trouble. An image entered my mind of the kid's face being disfigured from being burned with boiling grease, and Nelson winding up in prison. Luckily, his aim was a bit off and most of the grease missed the kid and wound up on the glass.

Nelson was impulsive, but he wasn't stupid. It appeared to me that he threw the hot grease at such an angle to hit the window. It provided the theatrics necessary to enable him to maintain his pride without actually hurting anyone. He was overpowered by the bigger kid, but he nearly burned his face and body. He threw the last punch! With the confrontation over, Nelson walked home with his dignity intact. I was left to clean up the mess of the spilled grease.

Nelson's next job after Jack in the Box was at the grocery store on 31st Avenue and 97th Street. The owner was an elderly Cuban man who seemed rather distant from the daily operation of the store. He left that to Nelson and another worker named Jorge. Nelson and Jorge became good friends and managed the store together, apparently sharing everything. I could never understand how two kids who worked in a grocery store were able to carry around wads of cash. They proudly invited Mom to a lobster dinner at The Buccaneer diner on Astoria Boulevard, almost on a weekly basis. Occasionally, they invited one or two of the siblings and friends. They impressed the girls in the neighborhood with their generosity. Mom never questioned it, preferring to act as if she did not know that Nelson and Jorge had a convenient piggy bank at work. The only saving grace for the unfortunate elderly owner was that, at least for Nelson, the job did not last too long.

CHAPTER NINE

☙☙☙☙☙☙☙☙☙☙☙☙☙☙☙☙☙☙☙☙☙

Father and Son

It is unimaginably tragic to lose a family member and not be able to pay your last respects. If we stop to put ourselves in the shoes of all the people who lost loved ones in war, or a terrorist act like the World Trade Center disaster in New York City on 9/11/2001, perhaps we could imagine the endless grief that not saying good-bye feels like. On September 19, 1972, Mom received a phone call with a message for Nelson on the other end: his biological father, Benjamin Marrero, had been killed when his car ran off a cliff in Puerto Rico. It was a Tuesday, exactly one week before his forty-first birthday. Nelson was devastated. He cried for days and would not go out. No longer would he be able to visit his dad in the Bronx, as he had done in the past from time to time. No longer could he say, "Hi, Papi," and hug him. No longer would he see his smile each time he visited him, or ask for his *bendicion* (blessing) when he left. There was never a detailed account of how or why his car went off the cliff. There were too many unanswered questions: Was he drinking? Was he with another woman and got distracted? Was the road slippery from rain? Did it happen last night or this morning? Did anyone find him? Where was his body? These were questions that had no answers.

Nelson was raised from birth by my dad, but he always had a close, very natural connection with his dad. Mom did a good thing in making sure that he knew who his biological dad was. It had nothing to do with child support, because Benjamin did not provide or offer any, other than giving Nelson a couple of bucks whenever he visited. It was simply that she felt it was the right thing to do. Her instincts were correct and well-placed. Nelson did not have to grow up wondering, like so many other children, who his real father was. He could learn and see through his own eyes how closely he resembled his dad: the hazel eyes, the wide nose, even his character as a womanizer. The few times I visited Benjamin with Nelson, I witnessed the attachment he felt. He showed elation when he saw him that he did not show with my dad at home. I thought, at the time, that it was unusual, because Benjamin didn't raise him or seek him out. It was Nelson who, when old enough, strived to stay in touch with his father. In retrospect, it was another sad story of a child who wished he had had more time with his dad.

And now he was gone! Perhaps Nelson cried so much when he heard the news partly because he knew he had lost any chance of attempting to get close to his dad. All the questions he wanted to ask him, but never could because their visits were so brief, so fleeting, could no longer be asked of him directly: Why did he and Mom get divorced? Was he there when he was born? Did he hold him as an infant? Did he love Mom? Could he go live with him?

It was disappointing and saddening to see how Dad became angered by Nelson's demonstration of grief over the loss of his natural father. I thought it was disrespectful, ignorant, and unnecessary. He yelled at Nelson, "Why are you crying? I raised you, not him," and "He didn't do anything for you all these years." I didn't think it was necessary to try to repress Nelson's anguish over the finality of his loss, which was horribly compounded by the inability to say good-bye. If Benjamin was ever a threat to Dad's psyche, that threat had vanished on a mountainside in Puerto Rico. If he could have thought logically, reasonably, about Nelson's loss, he would have understood that Nelson needed to grieve for a few days, a week, a month, and then would come to terms with the loss and move on. Even after Nelson stopped grieving outwardly, publicly, Benjamin's death would forever be on his mind. It would impact his life in such a way that he would try to make up for all the lost opportunities to make his dad proud of him. Dad's reaction only created another problem: Nelson's resentment of his stepfather. If I resented his reaction, I can only imagine how Nelson felt. It was Nelson's prerogative to grieve, and no one could take that away from him.

Nelson wasn't a confrontational person, despite his infantile antics. Nelson was developing a strong propensity for being irresponsible, but he had tender qualities, as well. I have come to terms with a better understanding of my brother, in hindsight. He wasn't a bad person—though many things he did were, in my judgment, so irresponsible they could have been construed as acts of a bad person. That was a misunderstanding of Nelson's fractured personality. He was misguided and needed focused discipline while growing up. He wasn't inherently sufficiently strong in character to overpower the weaknesses he was born with, and that were reinforced by the poor nurturing he received at home. Consequently, he didn't respond directly to Dad's insistence that he stop crying and mourning. How do you ask someone not to mourn? He didn't argue with Dad, didn't attempt to reason with him to let him grieve. He simply went on crying, even if he had to do it at night in bed, or walk out of the house. In a way, he was proud that he could look in the mirror and see parts of his dad in his own reflection, both physically and spiritually.

I was stunned when, a month later, Nelson announced he had enlisted in the Navy. I thought to myself, "He doesn't even know how to swim." He wanted to get away from home, but I thought his decision to go into the military was a hasty one. Walking by a recruiting office in Times Square, he was attracted to the uniforms the recruiting officers wore and the ones he saw on the life-sized posters. It was another impulsive move based on his attraction for the uniform. I am sure he didn't think it through to understand what he was getting himself into. It wasn't as if he craved more discipline in his life, or looked forward to the hard work in boot camp. He just wanted to wear the uniform. I dreaded seeing him go away. I was afraid he would wind up in the Vietnam War and I wouldn't be there to protect him. It made me numbingly sad that he wanted to leave us.

I wished to stay with Nelson as long as possible, so I told him I would accompany him on the subway ride to Fort Hamilton, where he was scheduled to begin his indoctrination process. The day he had to leave, we got up at 4:30 in the morning and left the house at 5 a.m. No one else got up at that time. My parents and Evelyn, Wil, and Susan said good-bye to him the night before. We took the bus from Astoria Boulevard to the Junction Boulevard train station, where we got on the Number 7 Flushing Line to Queensboro Plaza. During the trip, I told Nelson I was going to miss him.

"Take care of yourself and call us if you need anything. I wish you were not going into the Navy."

He said to me, "I know, but I will be fine. I will let you know how I'm doing out there."

We transferred to the Brooklyn-bound "R" train and rode it to the last stop. Once we got there, we hugged and said good-bye. I didn't want to let him go, but had to. I was so sad, feeling like I was losing my brother, for good this time. My eyes were tearing as I saw him walk away and as I sat on the train for my return trip home.

I was frightened that he might never come back, or that he would come back injured. I remember around that same time, I met a guy working at Jack in the Box who had returned from Vietnam and saw how messed up he was. Pat was very thin and nervous, always twitching and biting his fingernails. Sometimes when the store was closed at night, we sat around the dining room and he shared war stories with us. He told us about the constant bombings and how he had to hide in trenches, or underneath trucks, as the bombs fell with no forewarning. He developed a twitch which accentuated his nervousness. I could not even imagine the harrowing experiences he had gone through, but felt sorry for him because it seemed that he was a broken young man. He couldn't have been more than twenty. Whenever a truck's engine backfired on the street, Pat immediately ran for "cover" underneath a parked car. For as long as I knew him, which was about two years, this reaction did not subside. It was seeing how war had affected people like Pat that made me feel frightened for Nelson.

It was only one week after he left home for the Navy that we began getting a series of calls from Nelson. The first call was to tell Mom he was being mistreated. It didn't occur to us that he was at boot camp and was having a difficult time with the very structured and strenuous conditioning, both mental and physical, that is essentially what boot camp is. Mom and the rest of us at home were simply listening to Nelson's side of the story. In retrospect, we should have interpreted his complaints and calls for help as his shocked reaction to the required conditioning exercises. Even at that time, I wondered why he enlisted in the Navy if he didn't know how to swim.

He must have figured out after the first week that he made a mistake when he didn't consider that he would not be exempt from the drills to prepare him to be a combat sailor. He couldn't simply tell his superiors, "No thanks, no swimming for me." Mom told me she was worried about him because he told her they tried to drown him. Translation: he had to learn to swim. During his second week, he called Mom to tell her he got into a fight and someone cut him. Of course, we were many miles away and could not see what was really going on. All we had to go by were Nelson's pleas when he called.

I was frightened for him. I knew he was somewhat frail and was not a fighter. I had visions of Nelson getting beat up when he was unable to complete a drill.

When he told Mom that he had been cut, I took it upon myself to contact the recruiting officer who had enlisted him. I asked him to help us get to Nelson because he had called with complaints of fights and abuse. The officer tried to help, but I think he probably knew much more than he was telling us. He was probably thinking, "What did I get myself into enlisting this kid?" I must have called the man three times with my own desperate pleas for help to find out what was happening to my brother. We were not permitted to contact Nelson directly, but the recruiter tried on our behalf—or, at least, that is what he told me. He probably did get in touch with the base where Nelson was undergoing boot camp and was able to get his own version of what was going on.

The Navy boot camp website details the second week of boot camp as "confidence-building week." It says, "You'll be going through the confidence course, a course designed to simulate shipboard situations you could encounter in an emergency. Stay sharp because your life and the lives of your fellow shipmates depend on it. Teamwork and confidence are the themes for week 2." Again, we didn't know this at the time, as neither Mom nor Dad researched the process to enlighten and prepare Nelson before he excitedly boarded the subway with me on his way to Fort Hamilton. And Nelson either didn't look into it or pay attention to the recruiter when he was told what to expect. If week one was a shock to him, week two would be gut-wrenching. Week three would be hands-on drills on a ship, and week four would be live fire. Basic training would be over after eight weeks.

Nelson was determined to quit before he could get to the point of graduation. Military life was not for him.

I was desperately anxious and afraid for him, not knowing what they were doing to him. All I knew was that he was complaining that he was being mistreated. It all sounded scary to a fifteen-year-old. I had been protecting Nelson in the past from fights in the streets or school, but now I felt helplessly afraid for him. I had no idea where he was, so all I could do was call the recruiting officer and beg him to help us. Even if I did know where he was, I could not get on an airplane to save him. I wanted to know who stabbed him or cut him. Were the wounds long and requiring of medical treatment, stitches? He mentioned during a desperate phone call home that he had been cut on his arms. My imagination took control of my thoughts. Maybe the cuts were so long that he did indeed need many stitches. He must have been stretched out on a hospital bed. I hoped he hadn't ruptured a vein. Why didn't anyone stop the attack? I thought they were there to protect and care for the recruits.

I placed my third call to the recruiting officer. I wanted to know if he had investigated the situation with my brother like he promised he would. I remember that I couldn't sleep at night, worried that Nelson could be hurt or killed. The whole episode perplexed me. How could these things happen? How could the Navy and the boot camp people allow a recruit to be abused and endangered? I cried at night in my bed and felt so helpless that I could not go there to rescue him. The recruiting officer was no longer as responsive as he was in the beginning. He would not take my next call; that made me feel certain that the Navy was involved in the conspiracy to harm my brother. Did they want to kill him because he was not athletic and didn't know how to swim? Was it because he was not aggressive, not a fighter, and so they assumed he would not be a good soldier? Maybe it was because he was Puerto Rican? Mom had taught us that sometimes people might not like us because we were Puerto Rican. Maybe that was it with Nelson in the Navy?

It must have been around two o'clock in the afternoon on a warm and sunny day. I was walking down 94th Street in East Elmhurst in the direction of LaGuardia Airport. I had crossed Astoria Boulevard. My heart felt heavy with sadness for Nelson and the helplessness in not being able to get to where he was. My head was bowed as I walked, with no predetermined direction, figuratively and literally. I was just walking the streets. Perhaps subconsciously I was walking toward the airport to attempt to get to Nelson.

Almost miraculously, I looked up and my entire mood changed in the blink of an eye. As I tilted my head up from the concrete sidewalk to the horizon, in front of me, there he was. It was as if, on cue, a mystical sense pulled my head out from the ground to make contact with the vision of Nelson walking toward me, smiling as he saw me and wearing his Navy service dress blue jumper and white cover hat. I rushed to him and hugged him. I asked him if he was all right. He said he was and was coming home for good. In the instant I saw him, with that wide-grinned smile on his face, I sensed that he was proud that I could see him in his official Navy dress.

I was always curious and asking lots of questions, and this time was no different. I wanted to know what happened over there. Who hurt him? Where were the cuts he told us about when he called us, afraid for his life? The sleeves of his uniform top were hiding the scars, I imagined. How did they try to drown him, and who saved him from that? When was he going back? He appeared to me as normal and healthy as the early morning I rode the subway with him to Fort Hamilton. I was anxious for us to get back home so he could take off his uniform. I wanted to see the scars on his arms. I wanted to see if he had stitches, or how deep were the cuts.

When we arrived at our apartment, everyone was happy to see Nelson. Mom was especially happy to see her "baby" back. He didn't talk much about what happened to him at boot camp. I noticed that there were no scars at all on his arms. That is when I began to get suspicious of the entire affair. All of his calls were attempts to get Mom to extricate him from a situation he regretted getting himself into. He was too much of a free spirit to submit himself to a life of military structure and discipline. I knew from the day he announced he had enlisted that there was no way he would like having anyone tell him what to do, how to do it, and when to do it. None of us at home could stand that much structure. But I thought that perhaps he had calculated that it was time to change his ways and the discipline he would receive in the Navy was the best way for him to achieve that. I was wrong! Since Mom could not find a way to get him out, he made such a spectacle of himself at boot camp that he was dishonorably discharged. Nelson had again succeeded in getting himself out of a situation he had gotten himself into, but which he didn't like.

It was quite appropriate that even when dishonorably discharged, he strolled down the street, donning his sailor dress for all to see. He looked like a squeaky clean sailor with the bright white hat, neatly pressed navy blue jumper, bright white T-shirt peeking out from the top of his jumper, and shoes polished so fine he could have seen his own reflection on them. Knowing how impulsive Nelson was, I soon figured out that this is all he really wanted. He wanted everyone in the neighborhood—friends, neighbors, family members, and girlfriends—to see him in a Navy uniform. And now that he succeeded in getting out of his commitment, he could wear his uniform and tell anyone who would listen that he was in the Navy.

Other friends we knew who had gone into the military did so for vastly different reasons than Nelson. Sean, an Irish kid who lived on my grandparents' block on 92nd Street in Jackson Heights, also went into the Navy. Like us, Sean came from a poor family of five kids. He saw the Navy as a means of getting out of his environment and developing a career. I remember asking him during a return visit home how he got so muscular. His chest and pecs had grown large and were ripped. "It's just from swimming," he responded. I knew that Sean was athletic, because he and his brothers were always climbing the tall oak trees on the block. They would get so high on the trees that they got lost in the leaves and branches—until, like monkeys or squirrels, they gingerly crawled out in order to sit on the outer part of a branch. I was always afraid they would fall to the ground, but they never did.

Ray, another family friend from the South Bronx, enlisted in the Army. His motivation was to have a secured and steady income, as well as get away from the neighborhood. The block we lived on, Vyse Avenue and Tremont Avenue, had been deteriorating with gangs. Ray was a nice kid from a good family. His older brother, Pedro, was a close friend of my Uncle Mike's. I remember that Ray seemed happy to be in the Army. Whenever he came home for a visit, he stopped by our house to see us and always had a smile. Tragically, during a visit home, he was mugged in our building and thrown out of a hallway window. Ironically, he didn't die in Vietnam. He died in the neighborhood that he wanted to get away from when he joined the Army.

Whether it was a career, the security of a steady paycheck, or a way out of a bad neighborhood and its many influences, these guys—like I imagine many people who enlist in the military—had a long-term motivation that drove them to enlist in the first place. Nelson did not have the same vision inspiring his decision, however. Had he calculated where a career in the military could propel him, he might have endured the sacrifices demanded by boot camp. It was only a five-week process and he would graduate and move on to a full-fledged sailor; an accomplishment to be proud of. It was a shame that Nelson did not have the guidance at home required to temper and defuse his capricious nature. The Navy experience would have provided him with the opportunity to get the discipline he needed to become a more responsible, more focused person.

Since he respected Mom and heeded her advice and counsel, she would have been the best and only person who could have truly helped him stick it out to a positive conclusion. Unfortunately for Nelson, it was another opportunity squandered. Most everything he did, he quit before ever truly trying: the *bodega* in the Bronx, the paper route, the crossing guards at IS 145, Jack in the Box, McDonald's, high school, and now the Navy. It was a risky and unfortunate path that did not have to be that way.

At least Nelson was back at home where I could look out for him and protect him again. One evening my uncle, Aladino, who lived in the apartment next door to us with my aunt Irma and their two kids, Fofi and Sylvia, wanted Nelson to accompany him to JFK Airport. He worked there as a ramp employee and apparently wanted to go there to pick up his paycheck. It was about eight or nine in the evening in the summer. I was concerned for Nelson because Aladino was drunk, as he often was, and borrowed a friend's car to drive to the airport. I knew he didn't have a driver's license and had never before seen him drive a car. We were a pretty close family, and I would have known if he ever drove a car in the past. As a way of watching over Nelson, I convinced Aladino to let me go along as well.

Nelson sat in the front passenger side of the car and I sat in the rear. No one had a seatbelt on. Aladino was so drunk that he had difficulty seeing the road in front of his glazed eyes. Traffic was relatively light on the Van Wyck Expressway, thank goodness. The car swerved from side to side as Aladino struggled to control the vehicle. His vision was so impaired that his efforts were futile and dangerous for all of us. I was frightened for Nelson and me as the car banged into the concrete wall of an underpass. Aladino never stopped. He veered the car away from the wall and kept going. He then hit the median a couple more times before he finally brought the car to a stop outside of his job's office door. Nelson and I didn't say anything, but I could see the whites of his eyes, and he could see mine. What had we gotten ourselves into? We contemplated taking the subway back home and not getting in that missile of a car with Aladino behind the wheel. It was a thought that would prove prophetic.

Nelson and I waited inside the car as Aladino opened the trunk to remove something and went inside the office. It never occurred to me that he might have some contraband in the trunk that he had to deliver to someone. We never found out what that was, but I recall that he had once offered me marijuana when I was at his apartment. I wondered if that was what he was carrying. As we waited, I asked Nelson if we should take the subway back home. I was afraid we would get into a bad accident. He was afraid to leave, thinking Aladino would be angry with us. Besides, we had no money for the subway. I thought that was a lesser risk than staying and getting into an accident where we could be seriously injured, or killed. As for the fare for the train, I figured we could ask a stranger for help. It was about eleven in the evening when Aladino returned to the car from the office. It was too late for Nelson and me to leave on our own.

In his drunken stupor, Aladino deduced that he had locked the car keys in the trunk. For the next few hours, far past midnight, he tried, with our help, to unlock the trunk. I didn't know whose car he borrowed, but he would return it a completely disastrous mess. The driver side was all banged up and dented, and the rear seat ripped apart. He tried to get into the trunk from the backseat by dismantling it. He ripped the fabric cover off the seat and was able to see inside the trunk. The keys, however, were too far back, near the door opening. The metal frame of the backseat was not wide enough for him, or one of us, to get our arm through and reach the keys. The three of us tried virtually all night long, but our efforts were vain. None of us slept throughout that dreadfully adventurous night. Finally, at five in the morning, I stridently convinced Nelson that we should leave. We told Aladino that we had to get back home and were leaving. There was nothing he could do to stop us.

Nelson and I went inside the airport terminal to figure out how we would get back home. We didn't have money to call home, so we called collect from a public phone. Mom accepted the call, and we informed her of what had happened and where we were. She knew we had gone with Aladino, but was worried that we were out all night. In retrospect, I am shocked that she would not protest our going with him, considering how drunk he was. I suppose she was afraid of telling him that we could not go. Once we hung up the phone, we worked on figuring out our route to get home. We explained to a police officer that we were stranded and did not have money to get home to East Elmhurst. He was nice enough to let us ride the subway without having to pay, and we made our way home. We arrived at home around 7 a.m., exhausted, but thrilled to be home.

JFK Airport was perhaps fifteen miles away, but it might as well have been in another country. I don't know about Nelson, but I felt we were so far away that the thought that we may never get back home crossed my mind. Unbelievably, I heard through the family grapevine that Aladino was pissed that we left him alone at the airport. We were only teenagers and he actually risked our lives with his drunken driving, had us up all night when he locked the car keys in the trunk of the car, and he was upset with us! He didn't even have money to give us to get back home!

CHAPTER TEN

𝕊𝕊𝕊𝕊𝕊𝕊𝕊𝕊𝕊𝕊𝕊𝕊𝕊𝕊𝕊𝕊𝕊𝕊𝕊𝕊𝕊

Clashing Brothers

As Nelson returned from his short-lived military experience, he and I began to drift apart further. I don't know how he viewed our lives, but my observations showed me that we were very different individuals. Our approach to events in our young lives was at opposite ends. Our aspirations for our futures were as disparate as night and day, or as far apart as imaginable. I was focused on growing, learning, and forging a path that would help me to one day leave the neighborhood we were growing up in. My vision was very different than Nelson's impulsive and short-term way of thinking. I was more calculating and logical in my thought process. Most of the things I did, I contemplated a purpose and an outcome before doing them. When I worked as a teenager, it was a means of earning a salary, saving money for future use, and learning enough to achieve greater responsibility. I viewed work with a cause-and-effect perspective. I reasoned that if my superiors saw my initiative to want to do more, to take on more responsibility, it would eventually lead to a higher hourly wage, or, at a minimum, more hours worked that would result in a higher salary.

I saw that my motivations were totally opposite to Nelson's approach and his need for immediate gratification. Unfortunately, while I veered away from the manner in which our parents raised us, Nelson learned from their example and embraced it. As I wrote in my first book, *The Courage to be Different*, our parents lived day-to-day and never planned for the future. They did not encourage education, so dropping out of high school was easy and expected. They were always looking for help from others, rather than helping themselves. All five of us kids were obligated to be influenced by our parents' upbringing, naturally. But each of us was impacted by that influence differently based on our individual perspectives and our innate drives. I viewed what I learned in our home as how not to be, so I chose to be different. Nelson viewed it as the way to be, and it suited his natural desire for quick pleasure.

As we got a little older—Nelson, eighteen and I, sixteen—I saw that he was stumbling through the days without much of a purpose. I had dropped out of high school as well, but after two weeks, decided to go back. I went on to graduate high school and be the first one in our family to go to college when I enrolled at Baruch College, City University of New York. That period, from about 1973 to 1976, seemed to be the final turning point in our lives as brothers. Frustrated with the lack of guidance and support we received at home, I made a very conscious effort to focus on education as a means of elevating my social and economic standing, and a steady job to support my daily needs. Perhaps I was influenced by observing Nelson's life during that period, but did not appreciate it at the time. All I knew was that I desperately wanted to get out of poverty.

I was old enough to notice that Nelson's impulsive nature resulted in a demeanor that I felt was conveniently irresponsible. He had no patience for work, and no real desire to do so. Any job he got only lasted a couple of months. He spent his days sleeping late and then hanging out with friends. By this time, we did not have the same friends, so we didn't see much of each other. If he needed money, he would contrive a sob story in order to get it from his girlfriends or from Mom. He could always rely on Mom whenever he needed money. If she did not have money to give him when he asked, which was frequently, she herself borrowed money from someone else to give to him. If I asked her for money, she usually admitted she didn't have any and made no further effort to assist me.

At the time, I was disillusioned with Nelson's lifestyle and used it, among other inspiring experiences, as motivation to take my life in a vastly different direction. I thought that by going back to high school and on to college, I would be doing the right thing. What did not occur to me at the time is that just as I had been disillusioned with his lifestyle, he must have felt the same about mine, or, at a minimum, envious of it. We had become complete opposites. It was as simple as my wanting to be independent and Nelson leading a life of dependency.

In recent times each major holiday, like Christmas, Easter, and Mom's birthday, which happened to be December 22, Wil and I would gift cash to Mom inside a card. We knew that she could use it much more than flowers or some other material item. After years of following that ritual, which Mom both appreciated and came to expect, Wil learned something that he shared with me.

Evelyn, who had a proclivity for gossip, told him that when Nelson knew from speaking with Mom that either of us would be visiting, he would drive down from his home in Connecticut. His intention, however, was not to visit while either of us was at Mom's home. He waited in his car within eyesight of the building's front entrance. Once he saw that we left, he went up to Mom's apartment and she gave him some of the money. It might have been only twenty dollars, but it served his purpose of depending on others. It also perpetuated Mom's penchant for catering to him. This was happening well into his fifties. I thought it was devastatingly unhealthy for her to continue to treat him that way. She made it easy for him not to grow up and be responsible for himself. It was as if he was frozen in childhood.

Wil and I thought it was unfair that he should take money from Mom when she was poor and needed all the help we could provide. Mom denied that she gave him the money, which did not surprise us. She had denied things all her life in order to protect Nelson. Rather than continuing to give her cash each time, Wil occasionally had groceries delivered to her instead. That was the only way he could ensure that she received the full benefit of his support.

When Nelson was nineteen years old and out of work, he moved in with his girlfriend at the time, Luisa. They moved into an apartment in Corona, Queens, not far from where we still lived. The only way he and Luisa could carry an apartment was for her to work. Nelson had odd jobs, but nothing steady. On March 17, 1975, Luisa gave birth to their daughter, the first for each of them. They named her Patricia (Patty) Marrero, not so much in celebration of St. Patrick's Day—because we were hardly Irish—but in recognition of the holiday on which she was born. The relationship between Luisa and Nelson was a volatile one. Often he stopped by to complain to Mom about how poorly they were getting along. The fights, sometimes physical, were almost a daily occurrence. Eventually, and while Patty was an infant, they separated.

Our relationship as brothers had become quite distant as we ventured down different paths in our lives. The fact that I was going to college, working and earning a living, made me somewhat of a black sheep at home. At the same time, I was independent and had more resources than Nelson, and even my parents. I did not analyze the root cause of his behavior until many years later; in fact, not until our paths crossed again as he lay comatose on a hospital bed, but I thought that he was jealous of my independence and success. So much so that he attempted to take advantage of me for his own gain.

It might have been viewed as a minor, childish infraction the time he flipped the latch open to our bedroom door, knowing that I was in there alone with Robin. I felt it was disrespectful and rude, if not to me, to the sixteen-year-old girl in the room. He barged in with a devious smile on his face, as if certain he would catch us undressed and doing something forbidden.

"Hey, what the hell are you doing?" I yelled at him.

All he could say was, "Oh, oh, sorry."

I'm sure he must have been disappointed that he didn't see what he hoped to see. He didn't find any fodder for gossip when he rudely violated our privacy. I knew that if he had caught us in a compromising position, he would have spread the word among family members and friends, in hopes of humiliating me. He wouldn't have cared if he embarrassed Robin! He was too late. He was eighteen years old and should have known and done better. He should have been setting a positive example and been a good role model for us younger siblings.

Unfortunately, all he wanted to do was use people for whatever gain he could obtain for himself, and then discard them.

CHAPTER ELEVEN

🐢🐢🐢🐢🐢🐢🐢🐢🐢🐢🐢🐢🐢🐢🐢🐢🐢🐢🐢🐢🐢

Emotional Trauma

Did my brother and I become adversaries, embattled in a struggle of good versus evil? Or were we both victims of some affliction that was symptomatic of a serious illness, rather than evidence of a criminal nature? When I was in the midst of Nelson's destructive behavior and it was directed at me, my natural reaction at the time was to lash out in my own defense and protect myself. The last thing on my mind was to think that perhaps he needed, and perhaps was asking for, help. That was my parents', his parents' job. They should have interceded much earlier in his life to address the symptoms manifested in his behavior. There were plenty of opportunities for them to witness his erratic behavior and react in his best interest: when he stole money from the *bodega* at nine or ten years old, when he stole money from his paper route at fourteen or fifteen, when he stole money from the *bodega* in East Elmhurst at fifteen and sixteen—treating

Mom to lobster dinners at The Buccaneer diner with the ill-gained money—or a host of other transgressions that only showed his perspective that people were things to be used and then discarded. I recall telling Mom it was her fault that Nelson grew up to be irresponsible and troubled. I used to tell her that if she had put a stop to his destructive behavior early on in his life, he might have turned out very differently. He should have been treated, not celebrated.

What would inspire him to enter my bedroom when I wasn't home and steal my junior high school graduation ring? How much could he have gotten for it? Ten, maybe twenty dollars? Was that amount of money that important to hurt your own flesh and blood? No reasonable person, no respectful person—no caring family member—would commit such an offense. At least, that was my thinking. It just made no sense to me. Of course, by this time, I was fuming with anger. Still, he felt no repercussions from Mom and Dad, which further exacerbated my anger. I was just as angry with them for allowing Nelson to misbehave as I was with him. The only retaliation he endured was my yelling, but since he didn't seem to care, that was as significant as a fly circling in the air around him.

Nelson was the center of his own universe. The only thing that mattered to him was him. If he hurt someone else in his quest for pleasure or some sort of gain, so be it. I think he picked me as a target of his transgressions out of convenience. I was the only one, as the second child in the family, who had some cash in my pocket and a driver's license. He had neither, except for the cash he could get from girlfriends or from Mom. He knew how to drive a car, but never bothered to go through the process of obtaining a driver's license legally, until much later in his life.

I just felt betrayed, humiliated, and taken advantage of by Nelson. At the same time, I was confused, wondering how my own brother could do me so much harm. Initially, I was sure there was a mistake when I received a notice in the mail from the DMV Traffic Violations Bureau. They had suspended my driver's license for failure to pay a list of about nine tickets for various infractions. The summonses ranged from parking at a hydrant, to driving through a stop sign, to doing 79 miles per hour in a 55 MPH zone. I was sure that they had made a mistake. I contacted the TVB to let them know of the mistake, which I assured the clerk it must have been, since I had never even gotten a parking ticket up to that point in my driving experience. I was a careful and law-abiding driver.

The clerk, in turn, assured me that the summonses were in my name and suggested I go to the bureau and they could provide a printout of all the tickets. I had to go to the Department of Motor Vehicle's Traffic Violations Bureau on Veterans Highway in Hauppauge, New York, in order to get the details of the summonses. Traveling back and forth from there gave me ample time to think how this might have happened. Back then, in the 1970s, a New York State driver's license was comprised of two parts that were perforated, so that the renewal section could be easily separated when it came time to submit it and have the license renewed. Having been convinced by the authorities at the DMV that the tickets were indeed in my name, but knowing I didn't commit the infractions, I needed to determine how someone could have identified themselves as me while driving recklessly.

I reached into my pocket and pulled out my wallet to inspect my driver's license. It appeared to be intact, but then I noticed the renewal card was missing. Still, that didn't seem to me to be the reason for my troubles. It was just the renewal section, used for that purpose only, so a police officer would not accept it as evidence of a license to drive, or so I thought. Then I thought further: How could I be missing the renewal card? When could it have been stolen? My wallet is always in my pocket, except when I am at home in my room.

"Hmm, how could it have been stolen from my room?"

That's when it struck me! Nelson had previously stolen my junior high school graduation ring. I was so upset by that violation of my privacy that I didn't bother to check all my belongings carefully enough to ensure all else was in its place. I did look in my wallet at the time, but noticed that things seemed in order, including my driver's license. But, what I saw was the actual license and did not see the renewal card, but didn't think anything of it at the time. By this process of deduction, I was certain that it was Nelson who used my driver identification to impersonate me while driving and amassing summonses.

I went home with my printout of the summonses and confronted him in front of Mom. I expected an argument, a denial, and indignation at my accusation. I got none of that. Instead, to my astonishment, Nelson admitted it. Although I was relieved that I found out who the culprit was, it was disturbing to watch him admit to what amounted to criminal behavior without the slightest expression of remorse. He never apologized, and didn't offer an explanation as to why he did it. Even worse,

Mom did not reprimand him. It was as if she was okay with his behavior. That infuriated me. In my haste to get this issue behind me and have my license reinstated, I never asked him why he did it. I should have, because I have always been curious why Nelson did this and many other things. At the time, that was not important to me, however. Knowing how irresponsible and unreliable he was, my focus was to get him to the DMV bureau to pay for the tickets, admit his guilt before an officer there, and have my license reinstated.

I did feel surprised at how easily he admitted guilt and actually handed to me the renewal part of my license, with Mom standing in the room. She saw the entire exchange and didn't offer any lecture, request an apology from him to me, and did not scold him at all. This was just another example of Nelson's destructive actions without the introduction of a repercussion. There was no attempt to correct his behavior.

I was sure that he got the money to pay for the summonses from a girlfriend, but I didn't care. He went to the DMV with me, admitted that he impersonated me in piling up the summonses, paid for them, and we were done, for the time being. Even though I was angry with Nelson, I was just as angry with my parents for once again not disciplining him. How could he ever learn right from wrong if they never taught him the difference? Who was going to hold him accountable for his actions? He seemed to thrive in doing things that brought him pleasure or some sort of gain at someone else's expense, which he did not feel any remorse over. By this time, our relationship as brothers was extremely strained, bordering on estrangement. I loved my brother, but I didn't like him. I cared for him, but I didn't respect him.

Again, it did not occur to me at the time that my not questioning him further would come back to haunt me. I should have asked him why he did what he did. I should have asked more questions. So it was a few years later when I was stopped by the campus police at Stony Brook University, after inadvertently driving through a stop sign that was hidden behind overgrown tree branches, that I would feel Nelson's sting again. Once more my license, according to the police officer who stopped me, was suspended. It was for failure to pay moving violations summonses. I just knew that Nelson had done it again! Now I knew that he had so easily handed me the renewal portion of my license because in all his cynicism, he no longer needed it. He somehow used it to get a duplicate made. Sadly, he did not care that he was causing me so much damage and aggravation. He didn't care that I could be arrested, have my car confiscated, and lose time from work and school. Again, all he cared about was what he could gain at my expense. This went on for six years.

He never apologized. The second time, he again admitted to the offense and promised to pay the summonses. However, it got complicated when I wrote to the DMV Field Investigation Unit to report an unauthorized use or duplication of my driver's license. It was my attempt to get help in, not just reinstating my license, but finally bringing this type of violation to an end. I had to send the form to Albany, New York. I included copies of the previous offenses and their disposition as evidence that this had happened before and the court had acknowledged that I was innocent of the charges, and that the summonses were "actually issued to Nelson Marrero, who used Mr. Vicente's name."

The letter I received in reply said, "In order for us to open a case for you . . . you must bring criminal charges against your half-brother." That was the only time in my life that it occurred to me that Nelson was only my half-brother. I never considered him anything other than my brother. Still, I had to protect myself from any further damage from his impulsive and irresponsible behavior, so I proceeded to bring criminal charges against him. My parents would not do anything to stop the abuse, so I had to. I filed the complaint and obtained a summons, which I handed to Nelson. He was obliged to appear in court, surprised that I would go to that length to get him to stop. No one had held him accountable before.

At the first court appearance, while we waited outside the courtroom to have my case called, he looked at me and said, "You know, what you are doing by bringing me to court is hurting Mom. You are making her suffer by doing this."

I told him that I didn't care, that if he himself cared about Mom, he would not commit crimes. "What you did to me was criminal, and I will not stop until you go to jail."

After three appearances in court, each postponed because he did not appear with an attorney to represent him, as the judge had demanded, Nelson flew down to Puerto Rico to escape and hide. He saw that I was not backing down, and he must have felt he would finally feel the consequences of his actions. After so many years, someone was willing to hold him accountable for his actions. The judge issued a warrant for his arrest. I won the case as a result of his failure to appear, which facilitated having my license reinstated and the summonses dismissed.

The cumulative effect of the experiences was saddening, humiliating, and confusing. It was impossible for me to understand how my brother could hurt me so matter-of-factly. It was clearly something he did not care about. Did he hate me so much because I was different? Was he angry that I chose a path to my life that was contrary to his? Or was he jealous and envious of my achievements and my ambitions? Whatever the reasons, I did not want to give him any further opportunities to wound me.

CHAPTER TWELVE

🐝🐝🐝🐝🐝🐝🐝🐝🐝🐝🐝🐝🐝🐝🐝🐝🐝🐝🐝🐝🐝

Estranged

For the next thirty-two years, from 1982 to 2014, Nelson and I did not speak, except for the one time we saw each other when Mom was in the hospital in 2010. Mom tried to convince me to invite him to gatherings at my home whenever I hosted a holiday event or a birthday party, but each time, I refused. Evelyn and Susan did the same, but I refused their requests as well. Wil knew that I would not budge and respected my point of view, so he never tried to convince me to invite Nelson to my home. I was angry and wounded, but my decision was also, unfortunately, prudent for my own security. I did not trust him. If he visited my home, would he steal something? Perhaps I was paranoid, but given the history we had I preferred not to take the chance. I felt I had to protect myself and keep him away from me. Mom and my sisters found my fears groundless because he was "my brother." They thought I had overacted. Given the history of his actions, I felt completely justified in my decision and would not be swayed.

Even though I was angry, it was sad for two brothers who played together as children, went to school together, and slept in the same room for years to grow apart as much as Nelson and I did.

For more than three decades, I have searched to understand how we could grow up to be so different. Being a rather logical person, I could not accept that there was no rational, psychological explanation why two brothers who grew up as close as we did would grow up to be complete polar opposites and cause so much pain to each other and our family. Was it simply because we had different fathers?

Initially, I didn't consider that this could be a contributing factor, since Nelson was raised from birth by my dad. It was later, as an adult, and with a better understanding of the importance of genes in our personalities, that I reasoned this could be a cause. Was it damage caused to his brain when he hit his head on the manhole cover so many years before? I used to say, half-jokingly, that Nelson was never the same after that accident.

It's amazing to me how siblings can grow up in the very same home environment, yet turn out so differently. Nelson was a passive person and so tended to run away from situations that he didn't like. I had a stronger personality and didn't shy away from a fight of any kind. I believe this difference in our personalities, which was a natural trait each of us was born with, made a big difference in how we grew up. His weakness in personality, stoked by Mom's preferential treatment of him and lack of discipline, gave him all he needed to grow up as a dependent child and adult. He learned that if he didn't have money to eat or to pay the rent, Mom would take care of it. If Mom did not have money when he needed it, he was adept at extending his dependency to others. I discovered early in my life that I preferred to be independent. I never wanted to rely on anyone for anything. I had a competitive nature that drove me to want to succeed, initially to feed my ego, and later in life to ensure that I would be self-sufficient.

I remember telling a friend, Maria Pagan, one afternoon while we stood on the terrace of my studio apartment in Flushing, Queens, that I was going to be a millionaire one day. We were both around twenty-four years old at the time and talking about things we wanted to achieve. I remember her saying that she was confident I would accomplish that, because I always seemed to do whatever I set my mind to. I think about that conversation with Maria from time to time when I wonder what Nelson might have achieved had his life turned out differently. It saddens me to see him now lying in a hospital bed in a coma for the past five months, knowing that the many years we have been estranged are lost. It is time that we can never regain to patch up our early life differences and be loving brothers, supportive of each other. I can't help but wonder, "What if I had been a mentor to him, even though he was my older brother?" Could I have been a positive influence on him? Could I have helped him be successful in what he aspired to do in life?

My other siblings were somewhat of a grapevine of information over those years for each of us. Somehow, this kept Nelson and me at least aware of where we each were in life. We were still around each other in Corona and Flushing, Queens, when my daughter, Janie, was born in November of 1977. His first daughter, Patty, was two years old at that time. I still remember when his second child, Nelson Junior, was born to his then new wife, Morena. The next time I saw either Patty or Nelson Junior was at the hospital in New Britain, Connecticut, visiting their father in 2014. They were adults with spouses and children of their own. It was indeed bittersweet to see them under the circumstances. I couldn't help thinking that I could have been a better uncle to them over the years.

During one of my hospital visits, I met for the first time another of Nelson's daughters, Sue Ellen. Her mother, Demaris, was Nelson's third wife. I also met Angela, his eighteen-year-old daughter with his current wife, Maritza, whom he has been married to for the past twenty-four years. I was actually pleasantly surprised to learn that Nelson had settled down with Maritza after so many unsuccessful relationships that resulted in six children from five different wives, some common-law and some formal. His marriage to Maritza was formal and resulted in a son, Benjamin, so named after his paternal grandfather, and Angela—eight biological children. Nelson also had a stepdaughter, Maritza's oldest daughter, Jackie and a stepson, Dante.

Over the years, either Wil or Susan would tell me each time Nelson fathered another child. Three of his male children were named Nelson. I thought it must have been confusing for the three of them growing up with the same first name. I also thought it reflected my brother's narcissistic personality, which I came to believe was unhealthy and the cause of his difficulties in life.

His eight children, who included Patricia, Nelson II, Nelson III, Nelson IV, Maria Victoria, Angela, Sue Ellen, and Benjamin, were the product of his need to parade his virility to the world he lived in. Sadly, once the children were born, he did not stick around long enough to help raise them, except for his children with Maritza-Angela and Benji.

Both of us missed out on so many experiences that I'm sure would have fortified our bond as brothers, had we been able to share them. I know that because all the moments that Wil and I shared over the years only brought us closer together. As brothers, through the many experiences we shared, we have been able to understand each other as adults, from our likes and dislikes, to our priorities in life. Life, of course, is an ever-evolving journey. It requires constant fine-tuning along the way. I have found it to be invaluable to have a brother like Wil, whom I could share my most personal feelings with and listen to his, without the fear that either of us would have an ulterior motive. We trusted each other unconditionally and never had that trust betrayed.

When Wil got into trouble on the streets of Queens when he injured another kid, I made sure I was there to help him through that time. He was a teenager with a hot temper and got into an argument over his girlfriend, Grace. The argument escalated into a fight and Wil hurt the kid. Word got to me through other friends of Wil's. I let him know that it was wrong for him to have done what he had done and that he was lucky the other kid was not seriously wounded. I needed him to know that he was jeopardizing his life and his future. It wasn't worth it. I knew that I did not have a positive role model at home growing up, in either my dad or Nelson, and if I could mentor and be a positive influence on my younger brother, I was eager and happy to serve in that role.

When Wil was old enough to work and I was working as a software developer at Cushman and Wakefield in New York City, I was able to get him hired as a computer operator. That gave him his start in the technology field. He has always told me that he was glad he had me as a role model. He looked up to me and wanted to follow in my footsteps. He subsequently returned to high school after dropping out, as I and our other siblings had done, and graduated. He sacrificed mightily to attend New York University while working a full-time job, and graduated from there as well. The only ones in the family to attend his graduation were Janie, whom Wil was godfather to, and me. It gave me such a thrill to share in that significant accomplishment. It was also a positive influence on Janie, who went on to attend Rutger's University and graduate in four years. The three of us celebrated Wil's accomplishment with a nice lunch at Mario Batali's Babbo restaurant in New York City.

When my marriage to Daisy Nieves ended in divorce, Janie and I moved to New Jersey, Wil was the first person to come out from Queens and spend some time with us. I was despondent and depressed, and his visit helped to get me through those initial days as I resumed my life as a single dad. Wil was sufficiently sensitive to visit alone without his girlfriend and I appreciated that, although I would not have minded if he brought her as well.

Each Christmas, we gathered as a family at my home in New Jersey, sans Nelson. On my credenza in my writing office stands a picture from one of those holiday celebrations. I look at it and see standing Mom; Janie; my nieces, Jasmine and Priscilla; my sister, Susan; and Wil. Seated in front of them are nephews Luisito and Steven;

my sister, Evelyn; and Wil's wife at the time, Christina. I am seated to the left of them. Dad didn't like parties and complained that he got carsick, so he did not attend. And, regrettably, Nelson was not invited. I look at that picture and wonder what might have been if he and I had patched up our differences. He should have been in that picture.

When we were single, Wil and usually I went out on New Year's Eve to celebrate at a club. We smoked cigars, drank too much, and recounted the year's accomplishments, disappointments, and what we hoped to achieve in the New Year. It was at one of these celebrations at which Wil met Christina. Having celebrated at the Copacabana in New York City the previous year, we wanted a change of venue. We settled on a club on Long Island that a friend of Wil's knew. Just a few minutes before midnight struck, Wil and Christina's eyes met and they spent the rest of the night dancing and drinking. They dated for about a year before deciding to marry. Wil asked me to be his best man, which, of course, I was delighted to oblige him in. We had developed an inseparable and unbreakable bond as brothers. It was an honor to serve as his best man.

After his marriage to Christina dissolved, Wil and I took a trip to Cancun, Mexico, to spend a week away from everything. It was the first time we had taken a trip out of the country together. Every part of that trip, from the walk through the airport, which was interrupted by business calls, to the plane ride, and the week we spent on the beach, was memorable—just two brothers having a good time together. We were going to treat ourselves very well on that trip. We checked into a suite at the JW Marriott, complete with a hot tub on the terrace overlooking the sapphire blue Caribbean Sea. We played golf, smoked cigars poolside, and imbibed in fruity cocktails and Tecate beer by day. At night, we headed over to the dance club located in the Krystal Hotel, or the Latin club down the street.

Over the years, life's trials and tribulations tested that bond, but could never break it. When Wil was younger, I could influence his direction by simply telling him what was right and what was wrong. At a certain point in his adult life, that was no longer effective. He was his own man, successful in many ways, and didn't need me playing a father figure any longer. I had to adjust my approach to be more sensitive in offering my advice and opinion. He did the same with me. We were no longer older and younger brother. We were adults dealing with life and being supportive of each other along the way as needed.

Nelson was such a happy-go-lucky guy that I am certain we would have had a wonderful time if he joined us on these adventures, if circumstances had been different. But it was not meant to be.

In many ways, we both succeeded in leaving behind a troubled home and abusive family life. In all my naiveté, I assumed that in becoming educated and financially successful, I could forget about my past. One of the many lessons I have learned in my life is that blood is thicker than water and family, for better or worse, is forever. Eventually, we all have to come back home, one way or another, in order to truly be at peace. Nelson and I have been estranged for thirty-two years, yet seeing him for the first time after so many years in a hospital bed feels as if I just saw him yesterday. He was my brother when we were infants and is still my brother today. It is an absolute shame that he never realized how important that relationship is and wound up abusing it.

His greatest love in life was not his children or his wife. In fact, once he got divorced, he lost touch with his children of that marriage. Susan told me, recalling a conversation she had with him before his accident, that he regretted not being in communication with his children. He wanted to rectify that and see them more frequently. One of the Nelson boys was in prison in New York and the rest of his children were scattered throughout the boroughs of the city and Florida. Susan attempted to have the prison grant permission for Nelson III to see his dad at the hospital, but was denied. They would have granted him permission if his dad was in a hospital in New York, but could not transport him across state lines into Connecticut.

His most recent son with Maritza died on November 15, 2009, at the age of eighteen. I never asked Maritza how, especially now that she was managing through Nelson's medical condition, but everyone else in the family told me that Benji contracted AIDS at birth and that was the cause of his death. The family grapevine asserted that Maritza had HIV and they assumed, with no medical affirmation, that Nelson had HIV as well. I recall that I had heard this story several times over the years from Evelyn. She would interject in a totally unrelated conversation that Nelson was infected with the virus. She told me, "You know, Nelson has AIDS. He got it from Maritza." That gossip, whether the allegation was true or not, reverberated throughout the extended family. In casual conversation, Mom repeated it, telling me, "Nelson has AIDS." They never bothered to ask either Nelson or Maritza directly.

During a phone conversation with a nurse at the hospital where Nelson was being treated and cared for, the nurse mentioned to me that my cousins, Daisy and Rosie, had been visiting him that afternoon. She was alarmed that they were the first to inform her, or anyone else at the hospital, that Nelson had AIDS. It was upsetting, but not surprising (given the gossip-mongers that they were) that they would share unsubstantiated medical history to his attending nurse. She asked me if I knew.

I told her that I had heard that previously, but had no way of corroborating it. "Why don't you just test him? You have him right there at the hospital."

"We did," she said.

"And…?"

"It was negative."

"Well, there's your answer." I apologized to her on behalf of the family and asked Maritza to please keep the visiting for Nelson to herself, her kids, and his mother and us siblings. We needed to keep the gossip-mongers and disingenuous thrill-seekers away.

It gave me great pleasure to inform Evelyn that Nelson, contrary to her disseminated information, did not have AIDS or HIV. Susan was happy to hear the news as well, fully and officially corroborated by a hospital who administered the test.

"I'm so happy that at least it sets the record straight," she said.

The implication was that when he dies, his name will be cleared, at least of that untruth. I was happy about that as well. I've never liked the spreading of rumors and innuendos that some family members seemed to revel in. I found that practice to be malicious and hypocritical.

Chapter Thirteen

Cause

For years, even while we were estranged, I contemplated what could be the cause of Nelson's destructive and irresponsible behavior. I could not accept that he was of such a depraved nature as to conceive and carry out plots to hurt people. I especially could not accept that he despised me so much that he deliberately stole from me and impersonated me in amassing traffic violations that caused me so much aggravation with the law. I felt there was some root cause that would explain Nelson's harmful and predictable behavior. If we could identify a root cause, perhaps he could be helped. It would be wonderful to see him lead a constructive, rewarding life that would make him a productive member of society and of his family. Plus, if we could patch up our past differences, without fear of recurrence, he and I could do a reset of our relationship as brothers.

I had heard over the years that Nelson had become a successful Latin singer, and I was glad to hear that he was doing something he loved. I thought that he might have enough talent to be successful, not just in terms of singing at different venues, but in earning a reasonable living. He had told people many times that singing was his first love and it was all he wanted to do. He didn't want to work at a regular 9 to 5 job, and conveniently decided to go on disability due to his heart condition. That allowed him more time to focus on his singing. I have always felt that if someone wanted to work, they would do so despite almost any disability. There are many people who have heart problems or other chronic ailments and still manage to work and have a career. I myself suffered a heart attack in 2012 and returned to work on a light schedule in three days, and then full time within two weeks. Former Vice President Dick Chaney has had numerous heart procedures and always worked. Besides, I thought that the energy expended rehearsing and singing at the many venues Nelson attended was far more strenuous on the heart and body than any normal job he could have. So with his medical condition providing a pass from having to explain to anyone why he did not want to work, he was free to focus on his musical life.

The wrestler Chief Jay Strongbow, who Nelson and I saw back in the 1970s wrestling at Madison Square Garden, and who Nelson emulated when he played wrestler at the Lost Battalion on Queens Boulevard, provided a curious inspiration for his future. He became known locally and in Puerto Rico as El Cacique, the moniker he chose as his stage name. A *cacique* is an Indian chief in the Taíno native culture of Puerto Rico, as well as other Caribbean islands they inhabited, including Cuba, Jamaica, Hispaniola (presently Haiti and the Dominican Republic), in the Greater Antilles, the northern Lesser Antilles, and the Bahamas, where they were known as the Lucayans. They spoke the Taíno language, one of the Arawakan languages. On stage, Nelson wore a full-length traditional American Indian colorful feathered headdress, even though a *cacique* in Puerto Rico in the fifteenth and sixteenth centuries did not, and he was introduced as "El Cacique, Nelson Marrero."

The Indian headdress provided the flair he felt he needed to be noticed by everyone—with red, white, and blue feathers from head to toes, along with a bright red, white, and blue suit that resembled the Puerto Rican flag, complete with the single star emblazoned on the back. That is why I said earlier that he was like a Puerto Rican Liberace and Hector "Macho" Camacho, who himself occasionally entered the boxing ring in a Taíno-inspired outfit.

Nelson was in his glory, doing what he loved. He traveled to Puerto Rico and made appearances throughout the island giving concerts, usually at outdoor venues where the local townspeople could see him without having to pay. To advertise his concerts and the CDs he had produced, he appeared on Puerto Rico television shows such as *El Mediodia*, the island's midday entertainment show.

I was pleased that Nelson was doing what he loved and having success at it, even though his success produced many fans, but not much income. It was temporary, because there was no master plan, no long-term goals, and he wasn't making much money.

Whatever he did make, he spent just as quickly. But money was not his priority, not what made him happy. Each of us decides how we want to live our lives. Some people must have a long-term set of goals to work toward—an education to facilitate socio-economic advancement, financial targets to become as self-sufficient as possible, and provide a comfortable future for their children, a career that provides mental stimulation and growth, friends to share life with and create lasting relationships with. Nelson didn't seem to need any of that to be happy. All he needed was to be able to sing his songs for an audience that could see him and applaud him. He didn't do it for the money. If he tried to live his life like I lived mine, he would have been miserable. Susan told me once that Nelson had said that if one day he died singing, he would die happy. That was perhaps prophetic. When his son, Benji, died, his music, he had said, was the only thing that helped him cope with the tragic loss.

I can't help but wonder what he might have achieved with his music if Nelson had the proper guidance to cultivate his talent. I think anyone would be amazed to see him singing on Puerto Rico television, or at a club in Connecticut, if they knew that he had no formal training in his craft, yet had command of the stage the way he did.

He wrote songs about Puerto Rico, and specifically about Guayama, his adopted rural town. In one song that he sang on *El Mediodia* and on a CD titled Nelson Marrero "El Cacique," he calls Guayama his town, and tells the town: "Don't blame me, beloved town. If I've gone away, I didn't want to. Life and destiny have pushed me away, my beloved town."

"No me culpes pueblo querido. Si me he marchado, no lo he querido. Me empuja la vida, me empuja el destino, pueblo mio."

Although he was not born in Guayama, he loved it there, and was quoted in local Connecticut newspapers as having been born there. It was his mother's hometown, where he visited often to escape whatever trouble he was in back in New York, or to bask in the friendliness of the people. It is easy to love Guayama. The town is simple, beautiful and laid-back. Everyone knows each other, and Mom's family has a long history there. With great grandma, Mama Juana, living to one hundred and six years, Abuelo Julio, her son, currently one hundred and three, and other close relatives in their nineties, the Vicentes have a long and present history there. The people are friendly and peaceful, a trait that is legendary over the centuries throughout the island as the mainstay of the Taíno culture. And the people of Guayama love Nelson.

Interestingly, Nelson never mentions a thing in his music about Dad's town of Mayaguez. I can't help but think that although he was raised by Dad, he never accepted him as his father. Perhaps that is why he often looked for, and visited with, his biological father, Benjamin.

We might not have been raised in the ideal home—certainly ours was a chaotic and abusive home—but we were raised as ONE family. Consequently, none of us four children who were born after Nelson and to a different father saw him as a half-brother. To all of us, he was our brother. I asked Wil once how he viewed Nelson. He said to me, "I loved Nelson as a brother, but I knew I could not be like him. While you had gone in a different direction and started to focus on education, exercise, and a better life in general, Nelson stayed the same—joking, happy-go-lucky, not serious about a job, and always looking for an easy way of life, and he was okay with handouts from anyone." But he was our brother.

Whenever he went to Puerto Rico, he went directly to Guayama. He never went to Mayaguez to visit Dad's family. I wondered if he had difficulty with being a child of divorce. Did he resent Dad replacing Benjamin as his father figure? It wasn't a subject ever broached at home, so perhaps Nelson, if he felt troubled by this, dealt with it in silence. Most of us at home laughed it off whenever he said he was the black sheep of the family. How could he feel like that if he was Mom's favorite child? If anyone was the black sheep, it was me for being so different than most of my siblings, or so I thought.

I grew up assuming that Nelson saw the rest of us as we had seen him, as a brother or sister. It was that line of thinking, or assumption, that made it so disconcerting and humiliating when he violated the brotherly trust I also assumed existed between us when he stole from me and fraudulently used my driver's license. It suddenly occurred to me one day that perhaps he committed those offenses because he resented me, the first son of the man who replaced his father. It did not help that physically, I resembled Dad, I thought. Could it be that all these years that I thought of him as my brother, he saw me as his half-brother from a different father, and he didn't like it?

CHAPTER FOURTEEN

✿✿✿✿✿✿✿✿✿✿✿✿✿✿✿✿✿✿✿✿✿✿✿✿

Role Model

"Nelson's expectation to get a free pass in life is something I couldn't understand anyone doing, and certainly not something I admired in him."

That is how Wil remembers his older brother. Older brothers usually feel a responsibility to be role models to their younger siblings. That is something taught by parents as they seek to motivate the older children to watch over the younger ones, especially in a home with five children, like ours was. Parents, by default, provide the initial reference of behavior and success for their children to emulate. They have a powerful, and natural, influence on what their children will become as adults. We can see that in so many generations of families where children follow in their father or mother's footsteps in their careers. The parents' behavior is paramount in how their children grow up to imitate them as parents themselves. This could be good or bad. Our parents were not the best role models. The examples they set for us were not the most positive. Living as poor as we did in the South Bronx, they were more concerned with what we were going to eat tomorrow than with what lessons they were teaching us.

My dad raised Nelson, but he did not seem to engage him in much for Nelson to feel close to him. Dad was not a father comfortable with showing his emotions. In all my life, I never heard him utter the words "I love you." I never heard him say that to Mom, or to any of us, or to his mother when we visited her in Mayaguez. He never hugged any of us. When I became an adult, we shook hands when I visited, as if we were distant friends just being polite, seeing each other after a long absence. By contrast, when I visit my grandfather, Julio, we hug and he kisses me on the cheek, and I reciprocate. Dad never took Nelson to the baseball games at Yankee Stadium that he took me to. Perhaps Nelson didn't want to go, but there seemed to be no attempt made to teach Nelson about baseball, or anything else. Perhaps Nelson never took an interest in sports because he wanted to avoid playing catch with Dad, or going to a ball game with him. As it was, Dad played catch with me only once in my life. He never attended a school event for any of us.

The social skills he taught us were not very positive ones, either. In all the years that he worked at the Sunshine Biscuits factory in Long Island City, he never aspired to rise to a higher level of responsibility or gain a higher wage. I suppose he accepted that he could not become any more than the laborer he was and could not get a promotion and a raise. He never talked at home about his job, his accomplishments, his performance reviews, his aspirations—if he had any.

Eventually, when he was in his late forties, he was fired. As Mom, perhaps indiscreetly, told us, he falsified the price of a prescription bill and submitted a medical claim for reimbursement for an inflated amount. It was discovered and that was the end of a job he had for as long as I could remember as a child. He never worked again. By the time that happened, most of us kids were out of the house, leaving at early ages, from seventeen to nineteen. I wondered how he was going to provide for Mom, who had never worked, except for an occasional part-time job. That, however, was not his priority. He was reckless and irresponsible, and Nelson had a sufficiently fragile character that he succumbed to what he was taught at home.

Were we supposed to emulate that way of life? Dad never sought to find another job. It was almost as if he was rebelling against the entire family. He had always talked about having us take care of him and Mom when we were old enough to have jobs. I guess his goal was to retire early and live off the contributions we would make to him and Mom. It didn't make sense to us, because he was still in his forties at the time he expected this. When the reality was that each of us had our own lives to support, he stopped working. He supported Mom from a minimal disability check he got as a result of a bad back.

Knowing that they needed more money than he was bringing in with the disability check, I often asked him when he expected to look for a job.

He would reply, "The doctor said I cannot work. I have a bad back."

I saw that he walked fine, sat in his rocking chair in front of the television fine, and didn't complain of pain. I countered to him that many people have bad backs and still work. That was not a debilitating condition, I felt, to keep him from working. I reminded him, at one point, about my own chronic back problems. He didn't want to hear it, though.

When I thought of my own back problems, I knew that my dad reached a decision not to work ever again. His back was just a poor excuse, but indisputable. It was just after Christmas one year and I was driving from the neighborhood dump site in Somerset, New Jersey, with Janie, where I was discarding our Christmas tree. I had been recovering from the flu and was still feeling groggy. In retrospect, it was too soon for me to be driving a car. I drove through a stop sign, not seeing it behind overgrown branches of a tree on the corner. Janie was sitting in the passenger seat beside me. I turned to my right and saw a white car coming straight at us. Immediately, I pressed the accelerator as hard as I could, desperately trying to cross the intersection and avoid having the car smash into Janie's side of our car. My instinct at that moment was to protect her. As I looked to my right, I could see the other driver panic as her eyes widened where I could clearly see their whites. I thought we had gotten through the intersection when I felt the impact behind us. I was relieved that Janie's side was not hit. She seemed to be ok, and I felt the same. The impact of being sideswiped spun my BMW completely around 360 degrees, and its result caused two disks in the lumbar area of my back to bulge. I spent the next year in and out of physical therapy.

I was out of work for a total of one week. The rest of the time, I went to work, and two or three times a week attended physical therapy in the evening. Painkillers helped me get through the day. At the time, I was working at a real estate company in their Information Technology department. Getting in and out of my car to get to and from work was quite painful, and I sometimes broke into a sweat from the pain. But I went to work. At meetings, I asked my colleagues to excuse me, but I had to lie on the floor. I participated in the meetings from that vantage point. I was grateful that my colleagues and boss understood my condition. I didn't want to miss any work, if I could help it. At other times, while at my cubicle, I worked standing up because sitting was too painful, even with painkillers. One day, the pain was so intense that when I arrived home from work, all I could think of was numbing the pain somehow so that I could regain a semblance of normalcy—even if only momentarily. I grabbed a bottle of Dewar's scotch and guzzled it. I didn't care that I was taking Meloxicam for the pain. All I knew was that it wasn't enough to mask my chronic pain, and I needed relief. So I had no sympathy for my dad professing that he could not work because he had a bad back. When he told me that the doctor told him he could not work, I asked him to give me the contact details of that doctor and I would call him to verify that for myself. Naturally, I didn't expect him to fulfill my request, and he didn't.

My nature was much more inquisitive. I could not accept what didn't make sense to me. If I was not satisfied with the help I was getting at home, I sought it outside. I relied on teachers, uncles, and other father figures I was fortunate to find in the neighborhoods where we lived. I remember that as we became teenagers, I was quite vocal in protesting at home when I didn't agree or care for Mom or Dad's behavior. Nelson did not do that. Instead, he isolated himself to create a protective barrier against the destructive care he received at home, and seemed to be frozen in an immature state.

Nelson needed a driver, a strong father figure to discipline him and guide him through childhood and adolescence. That was vital if he was going to overcome being a child of divorce and lead a productive and responsible life. Instead, he was raised by a stepfather who seemed to believe that, as long as he provided a roof over his head that was the extent of his responsibility. He didn't have to love him or show him affection, and he didn't have to set good examples for the kid to follow. If I grew up to resent the way I was brought up as Dad's biological son, what effect did anyone expect this to have on Nelson, who knew he was a stepson? Sadly, he followed in those reckless and irresponsible footsteps. My persistent curiosity leads me to ask if Nelson's actions were symptoms of a disorder that plagued him as a result of the duality of his misfortune: being a child of divorce and having an unloving, uncaring stepfather.

CHAPTER FIFTEEN

The Disorder

I could not believe that my dad would not make an effort to visit Nelson at the hospital in Connecticut. He lay there in the critical care unit, having had two brain surgeries after suffering two strokes, yet the man who wanted the credit for having raised him would not rise up from his rocking chair and make the trip from Astoria to New Britain to put a hand on Nelson, say a prayer, and wish him a full recovery—even if that was just wishful thinking. At minimum, he would have the opportunity to see Nelson one more time should he deteriorate further and pass away from his delicate state. The doctors had prepared us for that eventuality, informing the family that he was unlikely to recover. My dad knew this as it was relayed to my mom, and she undoubtedly, in turn, communicated it to him.

As the days passed and Nelson was not showing signs of recovering, I expected that Dad would not miss an opportunity to be there with the family. Weeks and months went by, and he still did not make an appearance at the hospital. I asked Mom, who had been at the hospital several times, when he was going to visit Nelson at the hospital. She didn't know. I suspected that she knew, but preferred not to say that he would not be going. Here was the patriarch of the family, the man who raised us all, including his stepson, Nelson, and he could not find it in himself to show a glimmer of family leadership. He could speak to the doctors, to Nelson's wife, Maritza, to his grandchildren, who were in and out holding vigils in the waiting room as they waited turns to visit Nelson, two at a time, in the critical care unit.

Finally, I called him. I didn't expect him to change his mind and go to the hospital, but I wanted to let him know that he should be there.

"Hi, Dad. When are you going to the hospital to visit Nelson?"

"I can't," he said. "I get sick in cars."

"Well, you should take some medicine and find a way to get up there."

"No, I can't. I get sick."

"You are his father, and he is dying. You should be there and see him before he dies."

He didn't seem to care. Over the past ten years or so, he had developed another convenient ailment that prevented him from traveling to family gatherings of any kind: no Christmas celebrations, no Thanksgiving dinners, no birthday parties, and no births of grandchildren. He wouldn't accompany Mom to the hospital whenever she became ill, or visit her when she was interned for surgery or observation. I say 'convenient' because it was an ailment that, while so debilitating that he could not see family members unless they came to him, had the finality that no doctor and no amount of Dramamine could reverse. Now, it was so debilitating that it prevented him from visiting his dying stepson. It was unfortunate and disappointing. He decided years ago to isolate himself from family and all humanity, except for sharing an apartment with Mom. Something happened to him that I will research to attempt to understand before he passes away. He is now eighty-three years old. His soul died a long time ago.

But after seeing Nelson barely clinging on to life, with machines to aid him in breathing and nourishing his body, I decided to spend the time necessary in an attempt to gain a better understanding of his behavior over the years before we became estranged. While I was interested in understanding what now amounts to the first half of his life, I believe that whatever hypothesis I could come up with would apply to his entire life. I concluded that, at his core, Nelson was a good person who, over the course of his life, did bad things. By simply focusing on his behavior and his poor decisions, it is easy to surmise that he must be a bad person. That would be too simple an explanation for his many transgressions. I felt driven by the thirty-two years we were estranged, and the seemingly lost opportunity to make up for lost time, to dig into why he did what he did and why he was the way he was.

Time heals all wounds. With my anger over Nelson's actions toward me receded, I needed to re-acquaint myself with him as my brother, each of us having missed out on many years of our vastly different lives. I smiled as I watched him in videos and saw him in pictures in full display of the one thing in life that he was truly passionate about: his Latin music. When I saw the video of the midday television show in Puerto Rico, *El Mediodia*, I initially turned it off. I was looking for videos of El Cacique, Nelson's stage moniker. When the announcer on the show introduced El Cacique as the next act to appear, I doubted it would be my brother, so I turned it off. I thought for a moment that Cacique was such a known name of the native Taíno Indian heritage of the island, the announcer must have been warming up the audience to someone else. I went back a few days later and restarted the video. This time I waited as the announcer did his thing introducing the day's appearances and enticing the audience, in Spanish, of course. He then said, to my happy astonishment: "Direct from New York, Nelson Marrero, El Cacique." I felt my adrenaline jump in anticipation of seeing Nelson on the screen. There he was, quite different from his current state, and the way all his admiring friends and fans wanted to see him again.

At that moment, I saw him as a star on television, and I was a fan. The only thing that fans care about is to see how he entertains them with his lyrics, his passion, and his dancing. We could marvel at his equally entertaining costume of red, white, and blue Indian chief headdress and his Puerto Rican flag-inspired suit. I could see, not just hear, the passion with which he sang the song to Guayama, "Mi Pueblo." A chill reverberated up my spine as I saw him sing that song on the video. It brought back memories of that summer in 1970 when Nelson and I spent time there visiting with Mom's family. The people lived simple lives, and were so friendly that it was easy for anyone to fall in love with the town. They touched our hearts in such a warm way that we were sad to leave and anxious to return. It was such a small town that everyone knew each other. Visiting our great grandmother, Mama Juana, was easily the highlight of my visit there.

As I watched Nelson's videos on YouTube and sifted through pictures of his younger days and more recent years, I felt an urge to have a better understanding of his behavior throughout his life. It became important to view his life on a more scientific level and not take things personally. Perhaps some of the negative things that Nelson did over the years were—as unfortunate and damaging as they were, both to him and others—a manifestation of a deeper problem in his life. Perhaps they were symptoms of a serious problem that had gone undetected, undiagnosed, untreated, and whirled out of control. In retrospect, it could not have been so simple as to have been a matter of convenience. He needed a few bucks, so he stole my class ring. Or, he wanted to drive a car, so he stole my driver's license and impersonated me. Why would that then give him the "license" to commit driving violations and accumulate all those summonses? It did not make any sense. Why would he father so many children and then leave them? It didn't seem logical to me that he would be so careless, so cold, as to abandon his own children as infants and toddlers. I knew that Nelson was fragile, even weak, as a child. He needed much care and attention. He needed loving care to develop into a young adult. He was not a violent child, and he was not a violent adult. So what was the root cause or causes in his life that made him behave reckless, irresponsible, and self-destructive?

The experiences he was exposed to as a child had to be at the center of his behavior, I thought. He grew up knowing that he was a child of divorced parents. He needed the positive and caring attention of his stepfather and his mother. Mom and Dad went on to have four more children, and Nelson was not helped in adapting to the growing competition for love and affection at home. That circumstance, compounded by Dad's lack of affection toward Nelson, created tremendous conflict within him. Imagine a vulnerable five- or six-year-old who learned that his father had left before he was born. It didn't matter if it was his mother who left his dad. Further, what did Mom tell him as the reason that his father was not the man raising and caring for him? Did she tell him that their separation was the result of irreconcilable differences? Or was it because they could not get along? Perhaps it was because he was not a nice man with her? Whatever the reasons were, they planted a seed that was a part of what his personality would blossom into. The famous psychologist, Dr. B.F. Skinner, wrote in *About Behaviorism*: "What a person is really like could mean what he would have been like if we could have seen him before his behavior was subjected to the action of an environment. We should then have known his 'human nature.'"

Nelson's nature as a passive, dependent, sensitive child was further conflicted by the fact that my father's own nature was devoid of the ability to openly display affection. Instead of a living and caring home headed by a positive male role model as a father figure, Nelson was shaped by behavior that was callous and cruel. This seemed to reinforce in him the feeling that if his dad, Benjamin, had abandoned him, it must have been for a good reason. He became closer with his dad as he got older, in his teen years, and at the same time became disconnected from his stepfather. At the same time, Mom overcompensated for the lack of proper caregiving that Dad offered by not disciplining him constructively. If he didn't want to go to school, that was okay. If he injured a sibling, that was excused. If he stole from someone, she said he didn't understand what he was doing. If he quit his job as a teenager without a good reason, he was never counseled on the merits of responsibility. If he abandoned a child he had fathered, no one sat him down to encourage him to be a better father. The lack of organization in his life, and the incoherent manner in which he was raised, created a fragmented life. I remember telling my mother that she had created a monster by not caring for Nelson appropriately. That was not the truth, however. Looking back on how we were raised and the role that both our parents played in the process, it is more appropriate to acknowledge that it was both of them who created, not a monster, but a severely dysfunctional human being, who yearned to be caring and cared for.

I made it my mission to understand what happened to my brother. I wasn't interested in making excuses for him—certainly Mom did that for far too many years. I simply wanted to be able to explain why he did the things he did in his life. I thought it might give his children, grandchildren, and siblings a healthy way of viewing his life, rather than blaming him for anything he might have done to negatively impact their own lives.

CHAPTER SIXTEEN

✤✤✤✤✤✤✤✤✤✤✤✤✤✤✤✤✤✤✤✤✤

Was it NPD?

It is the love I have for my brother that motivated me to explore the possibility that he might have suffered from Narcissistic Personality Disorder, to explain how he behaved as his way of surviving a troubled and conflicted childhood. His passive nature as a child did not allow him to verbalize the confusion and isolation he felt as the family grew. Instead, he internalized his emotions and withdrew from the family, except when he needed something from them.

The day Mom dressed him as a girl on Halloween when he was a young boy left an important impression on him. The flattering response he received from every neighbor and person on the street, mostly women, made him feel happy and loved. It was as if he was Narcissus himself, seeing his reflection in a pool of water. He fell in love with himself, and the sensation he felt, however temporary or trivial, in response to the admiration showered on him when he dressed up in a costume. It was the type of attention that he surely was not getting at home, especially from a father figure who was not at all affectionate or kind, and who could not seem to offer positive feedback, expressions of love, or encouragement to any of his children, biological or otherwise.

Recollections of this experience with that Halloween costume, as well as his karate suit, his Navy uniform, and his imitation of Chief Jay Strongbow with the Indian headdress, and finally his image of a *cacique*, raised my curiosity to find a root cause to understand and explain my brother's life. I thought I had stumbled onto something and researched the definition, symptoms, causes, and possible treatments of Narcissistic Personality Disorder, or NPD.

I found this definition on *Psychology Today's website under Narcissistic Personality Disorder*:

- Narcissism Personality Disorder involves arrogant behavior, a lack of empathy for other people, and a need for admiration—all of which must be consistently at work and in relationships. People who are narcissistic are frequently described as cocky, self-centered, manipulative, and demanding. Narcissists may concentrate on unlikely personal outcomes (e.g., fame) and may be convinced that they deserve special treatment.

Some of the symptoms listed by *Psychology Today* include:

- Reacts to criticism with anger; shame or humiliation

- Takes advantage of others to reach his or her own goals
- Exaggerates own importance
- Exaggerates achievements and talents
- Entertains unrealistic fantasies about success, power, beauty, intelligence, or romance
- Has unreasonable expectation of favorable treatment
- Requires constant attention and positive reinforcement from others
- Is easily jealous
- Disregards the feelings of others, lacks empathy
- Has obsessive self-interest
- Pursues mainly selfish goals

The publication goes on to say: "Narcissists are usually physically attractive and charming at first glance, so they may have advantages when they first meet people (making a sale, getting a first date, gaining popularity). However, the long-term outcomes of narcissists are usually quite dismal, especially socially (e.g., long-term relationship difficulties). On average, levels of narcissism drop off dramatically by age 30."

The definition and many of the symptoms above struck a chord with me. Having observed in Nelson, and been a subject of, many of the symptoms that describe NPD, I was certain this was what plagued him all the years of his life. The lack of empathy he exhibited when stealing from the *bodega* in the South Bronx at such a young age, or stealing from an elderly deli owner in Queens who was working in his later years to support his family, or stealing from me and using my driver identification to carelessly amass violations, and his inability to maintain lasting relationships with many of the women with whom he fathered his eight children, including Nelson II, III, and IV.

Nelson longed to create an alternate image to present to the world so that he was not seen as himself, but as someone else. He didn't think that being Nelson could satisfy his need for constant attention and positive reinforcement. Certainly, as Nelson, he didn't find the attention, encouragement, and expressions of love and admiration at home from his parents, especially his stepfather, so why would he find that from others in the outside world? But, if he was someone else—ultimately, El Cacique—people would find him entertaining and feed his hunger for fame and popularity. His lifestyle reflected his need for sensation-seeking and impulsivity.

I had asked myself earlier if his misdeeds against me many years ago were motivated, at least in part, by jealousy. At the time, and even years later, it didn't make sense to me that he would single me out to steal my class ring and money from my room at home, or take and abuse my driver's license in the malicious manner in which he did. But, when I consider that he might have been suffering from NPD, then the thought that his behavior toward me, in this case, was the result of jealousy, disregard for my feelings and the harm his actions may cause me, and his selfishness, then I could understand that it was more opportunistic than it was personal. He might have been jealous that I succeeded in getting a driver's license and he had not done so, even though he was the older brother. He might have been jealous that I was doing well in school and he had dropped out. He might have been jealous that I had a steady job and had been promoted and he could not seem to hold on to lasting employment. He knew that I had money because of my steady job, and he had to ask others for money—Mom, friends, and girlfriends.

Having investigated the characteristics of Narcissistic Personality Disorder as a condition that made Nelson unstable in his emotions, and fueled the development of a distorted self-image, I felt at peace that the harm he had done to me, and also to other people, was not personal. He had developed this condition and we, his family, and especially our parents, did not recognize his erratic, irresponsible behavior as a disorder that needed to be treated with psychotherapy. That realization opened the door for me to forgive my brother for his transgressions. A burden was instantly lifted from my shoulders. I suddenly could stop asking "How could he do that to me?" I could now understand what Patty, his first daughter, said to me. I had not seen or spoken to her in many years, but we were reunited by the recent health emergency suffered by her father. She knew that I had been to the hospital to visit Nelson, and called me from the car as she was on her way to the hospital one day. She asked me if I was going to the hospital that day to participate in the family meeting with the doctors, as they explored next steps in Nelson's care after the two brain surgeries that were performed. I told her that I would indeed be there for that meeting. Before she hung up she said, "Tio, I want you to know that Papi always loved you. I know that for a fact, so please believe me." Had I still been angry with Nelson, that would have meant nothing to me.

My natural reaction would have been to think, "Of course he doesn't love me. If he did, he would not have been so cruel to me." But instead, her words reverberated through me and touched my heart. I knew that the skinny little boy who I played so joyfully with and who I protected was not naturally evil. He was, like all five of us, a victim of the environment he grew up in. We were a fractured family! And so on one of my visits to see him at the hospital, I dressed with the requisite hospital sanitary gown, rubber gloves, and mask over my mouth and nose, gazing at him and remembering better days when we were kids while I dressed. I walked into his room and placed my right hand on his right arm. I didn't know if he could hear me at all as he lay there motionless, but I hoped that he could—that he knew his brother was there beside him, to protect him once more, if at all possible. I whispered to him, "I want you to know that I forgive you. I know you did not mean to hurt me. You're my brother and I love you."

CHAPTER SEVENTEEN

Regrets

I regretted that it took so much time, so many years, for me to come to the realization that my brother was suffering with an illness that could have been and should have been recognized, then dealt with. Time heals all wounds. It's a cliché, but like all clichés, very true, for one reason or another. In the case of Nelson and me, it took thirty-two years and his vegetative state for me to recognize that there might have been a deeper root cause for his harmful impulsivity.

In reading about the causes of NPD, I wondered: What might have happened if there was some intervention with our parents to help them improve their parenting? Perhaps they could have recognized early on in our development as children that they were causing irreparable damage to their own children.

Once I learned about NPD, my natural process was to study the symptoms, then the possible causes, and then available treatments. One possible cause of the ailment that struck me was that "narcissistic personality disorder might develop as the result of neglect or abuse and trauma inflicted by parents or other authority figures during childhood." My recollection of the trauma we experienced as children made that defined cause resonate with me. It was clear to me that the physical abuse we experienced at the hands of our parents was traumatic for each of us. Nelson had the added burden of being a child of divorce. He also had a stepfather who, as I have said before, did not show him the natural affection that a father and child experience. There was no bond there that nurtured his hunger for the warm embrace of a father, or the cuddle that would make him feel safe and protected. If Nelson felt rejected by his natural dad, he felt unloved by his stepfather. Our mom was at the other extreme, overcompensating for Nelson's loss of a father and an inattentive stepfather. She treated him as special. Nelson was her first child, and she felt compelled to disregard his early acts of selfishness and malice. Another psychologist I read said: "Being brought up without negative consequences for being selfish and hurtful creates a social monster." Perhaps not ironically, I used to tell her that by not disciplining Nelson for his misdeeds, she was creating a monster. Inherently, he had a fragile, delicate personality and the two extremes of caregiving by our parents—one overcompensating and accepting of negative behavior, and the other grossly inattentive to his emotional needs—served to reinforce and nurture his development into an extreme narcissist.

What might have occurred if things had been different in Nelson's development as a child? That is worth pondering, if for no other reason than to understand how to raise children today to develop healthy social personalities. It also helps in identifying other relatives and people in society at large who exhibit extreme narcissistic traits. If we can identify these social deficiencies in others, we will be better equipped to respond to them and not enable them to hurt others.

In my brother's case, what if action was taken beginning with that event in the South Bronx when he stole a bag of dollar bills from the *bodega*? He was only nine or ten years old when that occurred, so I assume he was young enough to be taught right from wrong and the consequences of negative behavior. When he came home with all the toys he purchased with the stolen money, Mom should have questioned him further and not let up until he introduced her to the so-called mother of a friend. Since the phantom lady was a stranger, she should have at least taught him that he could not accept gifts from people who were unknown to her. And with that as a basis, she would have gone with him to return the items to the lady. It would have made the experience sufficiently difficult for a young boy that eventually, he would have caved in to the pressure. If he failed to present the lady, which would have been a certainty since she did not exist, Mom could have then thrown the items away. I doubt that she would have ever found out the actual truth that he stole money from the *bodega*. The store owner didn't tell her, for some reason, and I didn't tell her about the incident I had with him when he told me he suspected Nelson took the bag. There wasn't sufficient, indisputable evidence for her to believe that her favorite young son would do such a thing. The only way she could have uncovered the truth was if Nelson confessed under pressure.

She should have been suspicious enough to be cleverly creative in her investigation. The very fact that a young boy would come home with so many gifts allegedly given to him by a woman that his parents did not know, in the South Bronx, should have raised all sorts of red flags. What if the woman—or a man, if Nelson's story was true—was molesting him? What if the person wanted to abduct him? What if they were recruiting him to sell, or take, drugs? Could the person be interested in staking out where the boy lived in anticipation of burglarizing his home? With any level of skepticism, Mom could have summoned the help of the police.

Even if she called them because of genuine incredulity over the event, it would have possibly scared the boy and left an indelibly positive impression. It is entirely conceivable that once they were called in to investigate how a stranger could shower a young boy with so many gifts, their training in pursuing the truth might have resulted in enough pressure for Nelson to divulge the true source of the gifts—the stolen bag of dollar bills. I'm pretty certain the police officers questioning him would have themselves suspected that something was amiss. To perhaps conclude the episode, Mom could have asked the police to confiscate the merchandise. Even if that was not the eventual outcome, the mere presence of the police officers at our home questioning him would have been a positive lesson in itself. Whatever he did, he was not going to get away with it, so it is not worth doing it again.

Policemen are good at helping parents teach kids positive lessons, and they are generally happy to lecture and mentor them in situations like this one. At such a young age, he should not have been taught that he could indeed be smarter than his own parents.

Whatever the approach she might have followed, Nelson would have learned a valuable lesson as a young boy. Possibly multiple valuable lessons! He would have learned that he should not lie, because our parents would be dogmatic in their quest for the truth; he would have learned that he was not smarter than our parents, they would search and find the truth; he would have learned that it was not worth the trouble to steal, because ultimately, he wound up with nothing if he was forced to dispose of the items; and, most importantly, whatever you desire, work for it and earn it. It would have been his first lesson in not using people for his own pleasure.

A similarly direct and inquisitive approach was called for in other situations wherein Nelson exhibited early signs of impulsive and harmful behavior. Another opportunity for our parents to respond to a teachable event was when he was fired from the paper route for collecting fees from customers and keeping the money. It was clear to me what had happened. Mom should have stopped Nelson in his tracks to dig into the events that led to his loss of that job. I always refer to Mom, because Dad was even more clueless and disinterested in mentoring us and teaching us right from wrong than she was. Mom was also the one parent whom Nelson either respected or feared.

She might have asked Nelson, "What happened to the job? Tell me why you quit?"

"The boss treated me unfairly. He was yelling at me and I didn't like it," he would have responded. It was a vague response, but he knew that she was accepting of his usual ambiguity.

She would have helped him immeasurably had she taken Nelson by the hand and said, "Let's you and I go over there and speak with the boss."

If I walked by the place to ask what happened to my brother, certainly she could have and, in my opinion should have, done the same. I was twelve years old and had the curiosity and the concern for Nelson to investigate the incident. Had Mom done that, she would have learned that Nelson stole the money he had collected from customers. That was another teachable moment wasted!

I can only imagine the positive message that would be delivered to Nelson with a different scenario: Mom takes Nelson by the hand and they walk to the storefront where the newspaper distributor works out of, he going along begrudgingly because he knows she will not like what she is about to hear. She meets the boss, who tells her that her son stole money from him. He had collected whatever it was—seven, eight dollars and change—and did not hand it in. The boss scolded him and had no choice but to fire him. At that point, Mom gives Nelson a valuable lesson in righteousness. She forces Nelson to turn over the money to the boss and apologize, an all-important humbling experience. Or, if he had spent the money, she enters into an agreement with the boss of the paper route to have Nelson deliver papers for free (without the responsibility for collecting fees from customers) until the money is repaid. It is possible that the boss would not have accepted such an arrangement, if he didn't want Nelson around his business, but it would have been worth an attempt. Another, but less favorable alternative, given our financial hardships at home, would have been for her to repay the stolen money herself and have Nelson apologize.

I would not have liked the last option, because Nelson would have felt that he got away with his misdeed by having someone else pay on his behalf. He would not have felt a direct repercussion for his actions. In any case, one of these responses would have been far better in teaching him a lesson than simply accepting his story, which is what Mom did. This consistently apathetic responsiveness gradually created a "social monster." It was like a cancer whose warning signs were ignored. It was therefore allowed to grow out of control until it consumed all of him. His new personality as an extreme narcissist enabled Nelson to mask the wounds in his inner soul. From the traumatic separation from his father, Benjamin, whom he grew to love and long for, to the negligent caregiving from his stepfather and mother, Nelson screamed for intervention throughout his life as a child.

It was because his deep emotional bleeding went unattended that Nelson attempted to heal himself. That is when he began to act out by doing things that were hurtful to others and to him. When these cries for help backfired, he found pleasure in them. He anticipated that he would be discovered behaving badly and that he would be reprimanded, paid attention to, and ultimately, embraced and loved. In the absence of that as a response, he found happiness in the material things, however small they might have been, that he got from others: The bag of money and the toys he bought with it, the few bucks from the paper route, even wearing the Halloween costume when Mom dressed him as a girl. His behavior and the benefits he enjoyed from them formed the thick, yet visible, scar tissues over his emotional wounds.

Once he reached his teen years, he was so out of control that it would have been nearly impossible to cure him. The time to have interceded and help him was when he was a young boy acting out. The wounds were still fresh enough that he could have been helped. It is a shame that he was not treated in a different manner to correct his behavior, to teach him right from wrong. It was so easy for our parents to write off his behavior as antics of a kid, but that was passive and indifferent. His actions required the diligence that is the responsibility of good parents. Most psychologists whose work on extreme narcissistic disorder I have studied believe that it is very difficult to cure someone who has this personality disorder and that "most behavioral clinicians have difficulty knowing how to work with one," according to one doctor.

Dr. Samuel Lopez De Victoria, Ph.D in his online post *"I LOVE ME!": A Q&A About Narcissism* wrote: "For an extreme narcissist to be 'cured' he must want to heal and be willing to admit he is unhealthy." Scar tissue, which I equate Nelson's extreme narcissism behavior to, renders a wound healed. By the time Nelson fully developed his new personality, it became his identity. He was not going to recognize that underneath the scar tissue lays a wound that needed curing. He was cured! That is why, as Dr. Sam, as he is affectionately called on his website, www.drsam.tv, goes on to say, "For most narcissists, that is simply too much to ask."

The psychotherapist says, "For an extreme narcissist to want to change there must be a gigantic and earth-shattering series of events in their lives to break them of their grandiosity, extreme selfishness, entitlement, and self-righteousness. Should an extreme narcissist be willing to be helped, the clinician must be skilled enough to find the wounds in his inner soul, help heal them, and replace them with healthy self-images and patterns for relational dynamics. The only kind of extreme narcissist that can be cured is a broken one."

I cannot even imagine the monumental task of attempting to get Nelson to sit down with anyone, professional or otherwise, and begin a discussion of why he did the things he did. That is precisely what his behavior required when he was a child. It is what was required of his parents and that might have been enough, as he had not yet fully developed into an extreme narcissist. He was pretty much training to become one. To have him sit down with someone and talk about his actions, the root causes of them—his feelings about his dad and his stepdad, his mom, and his siblings—would have been earth-shattering indeed. The scar tissue had become much thicker than the wounds it covered.

My deepest regret, especially now that I recognize that Nelson must have suffered as a young boy with so many traumas, is that no one in the family intervened to give him the attention he needed to repair his fragile soul. It's an absolute shame that Mom and Dad did not have the energy and attentiveness to help him when he was at the early stages, when he could have been veered down the right path and away from a severe personality disorder. He was as innocent and as promising as any child could be. He just needed guidance and discipline to develop into a responsible, caring, productive adult. It is such as waste of a life!

CHAPTER EIGHTEEN

Tragic State

And now with all the anger I felt for so many years dissipated like the hot sun dissipates the morning dew, I'm left wondering what might have been of my brother. For five months now, he has been in a vegetative state with no signs of ever coming back to life as he knew it. I asked Susan, how is he doing, since she stays close to him, visiting him just about every week. Sometimes I get a detailed response: "A slight temperature and antibiotics in case he has an infection", she says on one occasion. Other times, she may reach a point of frustration at not seeing the improvement we are all anticipating and she simply says, "The same."

I feel bad for Susan and have tried to console her, tried to get her to go on with her life despite the tragedy of Nelson's condition. She tells me how she can't sleep or eat.

"Every day is a nightmare for me. I have knots in my stomach constantly and can't seem to stop crying."

"Susan, you have to move on with your life. You cannot let this get you sick as well. Try to be strong."

But her personality is very different than most of us other siblings. She is the type of person who can be overcome by emotion to the point where she cannot function normally. Her only escape seems to be going to work, where she can cast aside, in glimpses, the hardship we were all dealing with. I say 'in glimpses' because even from work, she would send me texts with updates from the hospital as she received them.

"Waiting for the doctor to call me, but Patty (Nelson's first daughter) is on her way there," she texted as she updated me when Nelson developed a fever and another infection.

I knew she wasn't sleeping, because I could get a message from her late at night or in the morning before 7 a.m. The night she learned that he had developed the latest bout of complications, she notified me the next morning by text, "Good morning, Nelson was sent to the hospital. His heart rate was in the 160s and oxygen level was low—as soon as I get an update I'll let you know." It was 6:43 Monday morning. I just knew she did not sleep a wink the night before. As much as I advised her to step back from this heartbreaking situation and not let it consume her life, she was overwhelmed by it.

As a family, we have been blessed by relatively good health and longevity. No one in the extended family of siblings, uncles and aunts, nephews and nieces, grandparents, and cousins has passed away in the past thirty years, with the exception of Nelson and Maritza's teenage son, Benjamin, who died of in 2009. Naturally, we have very little experience dealing with life and death situations. Dad is eighty-three, Mom is seventy-eight. Both are in reasonably good health, despite their requisite whining. Abuelo is one hundred and three, still living in his Queens home, except for an occasional hospital visit to treat age-related ailments, like a bad hip that hampers his ability to walk. He is alert and always smiling. His mom, my great grandmother, Mama Juana, died at one hundred and six.

This longevity in our family has led to a level of complacency. We expect that we will live a century. When Nelson initially suffered the two strokes, we fully expected that he would come out of it and return home to a semblance of normalcy. We anticipated, and discussed amongst the family, that he would likely have a long and arduous rehabilitation process. We talked about how difficult that would be for him, given his low tolerance for physical activity, and that he would need close moral support from us throughout that effort.

We were still hopeful even after he had multiple brain surgeries performed and were told by the nurses and doctors that he was in an induced coma. We thought: How bad can that be if he's in an induced coma that they will take him out of in a couple of days, as they told us? Susan, Wil, and I began to be more concerned when the doctors delayed in reducing the sedation. We became quite alarmed when they finally removed the sedation and the coma would not reverse. It didn't seem like much of a consolation when the nurse suggested that it might take a few days for the sedation to fully wear off. First they raise our hopes, and then they douse them. Wil and I talked about it, and that was the time that we felt we lost Nelson.

Still, we all wanted to give him a chance to recover. Maritza, Susan, Wil, Patty, and I were united in our wish to give him time to come out of the coma. None of us wanted to contemplate pulling the plug on him, despite the occasional subtle nudging by the doctors and hospital staff to "let him go." We remained obstinately hopeful. Our hopefulness was reinforced in the beginning by the doctors suggesting that it sometimes takes weeks for a patient in a similar state to show signs of recovery. It was a difficult and confusing stretch of months.

The single dissenter among us was Evelyn. She was adamant that the plug should be pulled on Nelson and he should be allowed to go with God. She was so adamant that she proceeded to lobby to Maritza, Wil, and me in an effort to sway us to her side. Evelyn, the older of my two sisters and two years younger than me, is also afflicted with the narcissistic personality disorder. She is constantly preoccupied with her appearance and envious of just about everyone around her. She wants you to think that she cares about you, when, in reality, she uses you to get what she wants. Once she has gotten what she wants, she will speak disparagingly about you to others and discard you like a useless piece of paper. It doesn't matter if you are a sibling, spouse, a so-called friend, or otherwise related to her. Everyone is fair game for her torrent of abuse.

During our ordeal with Nelson, Evelyn spewed her venomous attacks on anyone who was opposed to pulling the plug on Nelson. The first to feel her wrath was his wife, Maritza. The fact that she and Nelson were married for twenty-four years and endured the daily grind that was life with Nelson did not count for much with Evelyn. She showed no respect for their union, instead acting as though she and Mom, as blood relatives, should have a more meaningful say in his treatment. The frustration of the legal reality that his wife had the ultimate say over his care, and whether he would be taken off the respirator, was like walking into a hungry grizzly bear protecting her cubs. Double trouble! At a time that called for family unity, respect, and compassion, she was insulting, disrespectful, and downright vicious.

Frustrated that she could not influence Maritza in the decision-making process of Nelson's care, she lashed out at her with this text, one of many we would receive over the coming weeks: "Maritza, Mom is very depressed after seeing Nelson," as if only Mom's understandable depression was more important than anyone else's, including Maritza's, who was managing the tragedy day and night. "He is brain dead because now he doesn't follow you with his eyes anymore."

She either ignored or wasn't aware of the fact that the doctors had performed an electroencephalogram (EEG) on Nelson and concluded that he had electrical activity in his brain, and therefore was not brain dead. She was desperately trying to frighten Maritza into making the decision that she wanted made, but that she had no authority to make.

Nelson had been moved from the hospital to a nursing center, Village Green in Waterbury, Connecticut, for physical therapy, and that is where the encounter occurred that resulted in this response from Evelyn.

"Nelson looks like a monster. Poor thing, staring, blinking, and in diapers is not a life anybody deserves. The losers who work there said the patients that are dying are the ones sent there and that is the section Nelson is in."

She vacillated between a feeling of victimization and aggressiveness, common behavior of someone with narcissistic personality disorder, and nothing was working the way she wanted.

She went on: "You have no respect for my mother because you see the way Nelson is and you don't even warn her what to expect."

The fact was that we all knew what his physical appearance and his condition were and communicated that to Mom, but her hearing about it would not have mitigated the shock of seeing him that way.

Then she turned to sarcasm. "Nice, keep him suffering, you're doing a great job. Just remember, one day it will come to an end. At the funeral you will have no say, because he is going to be dead. We will take it from there."

I wasn't sure what she meant by that. What were the mother and siblings going to take over at the funeral, paying for the service?

"Thanks also for telling them not to talk to any of us and that we have to go through you."

Evelyn was insulted that Maritza, at my request, was trying to put a semblance of order to the flow of information to and from the hospital and the nursing home. It had become chaotic, with multiple family members calling on the same day to ask the same questions. The communication was disorganized and consuming too much time of the staff. It would have been more effective for the family to speak to each other and to Maritza for updates, but Evelyn could not understand that. Like a true extreme narcissist, it was all about her. If she wanted to get an update, she should be able to call the facility or the doctor herself. After all, she felt she was his sister and therefore had that right!

Amazingly, she followed that with, "I don't know who you think you are."

Since she was not getting what she wanted, she ignored the fact that Maritza was Nelson's wife of a quarter of a century and half his life. She should have been grateful that he found someone who stabilized a part of his life after having had children from five different women. Luckily, Maritza was strong enough to ignore her and not succumb to her ridiculous and abusive behavior.

Feeling that she was getting nowhere in her attempt to use Maritza for her gain, she concluded her text message with, "I feel really sorry for you when it will be your turn to be in a dying bed. What goes around comes around."

It was a ferociousness that was inexplicable and inexcusable. How could she speak to the grief-stricken spouse of a dying person in that manner? Where is the compassion, the understanding, the kind words of support? Having researched the personality of a person with extreme narcissism, I knew that we could not expect those emotions from Evelyn. Life is always just about her. To me, she was predictable. Once you come to terms with the reality that a person is an extreme narcissist, you can manage a relationship with that person, although usually that means staying away from them.

CHAPTER NINETEEN

㊉㊉㊉㊉㊉㊉㊉㊉㊉㊉㊉㊉㊉㊉㊉㊉㊉㊉㊉

Who's To Blame?

Rather than uniting with the family during this tragedy, Evelyn was seeking to place the blame for Nelson's condition on someone. She wanted to know who decided to keep him on life support. Initially, she placed all the blame on Maritza. Since Evelyn was undergoing back surgery the same week that Nelson had brain surgery after the strokes, she was not able to be present until about six weeks after her surgery, when she was permitted to get into a car for the drive to Connecticut. By that time, she missed the dynamics of the multitude of meetings we had with doctors and nurses as Maritza, Patty, Wil, Susan, and I debated the difficult task of deciding whether we should give Nelson a chance at life or "let him go," as some of the doctor's intimated, but were careful not to recommend outright.

"Doctor, does he have a chance to recover?"

The doctor said, "He has about a ten percent chance to recover, but he will have a long rehabilitation."

We got the sense from the responses of some of the doctors and administrators, especially a social worker the hospital assigned to our case, that they didn't believe Nelson was going to recover, but they would not say that directly to us, making it more difficult for us to take on the responsibility of making a life-and-death decision on his fate. Throughout our meetings, they continually expressed at least a miniscule chance for recovery. We were unanimous in our decision that as long as he had as little as a ten percent chance to recover, we would honor that chance. That was how we came to our unified decision. Our interaction with Maritza was respectful, supportive, and consoling. We were in this together.

If we were to be blamed for anything, it would have been for trying to do the best thing possible for Nelson under the difficult circumstances. We certainly could not be blamed for causing his strokes, or delaying his trip to the hospital to receive the care he needed. We could only be blamed for attempting to give him a chance to survive. And it wasn't just Maritza, or any other subset of the group. It was all of us. But Evelyn didn't care to see it that way. She wanted to know who to blame for letting him live in the condition he was in when she saw him. After her tirade against Maritza did not work in her favor, she turned her claws on Patty, Wil, and Susan. Apparently, Maritza explained to her in response to her reprehensible text, that the three of them voted to keep him on life support. Somehow, either Maritza forgot to mention me, or Evelyn, in her excitement at having fresh targets to attack, missed hearing my name.

We received a gruesome picture from her of Nelson lying in his hospital bed, as if we hadn't seen him that way on our visits, along with a note that partially said, "Here is a picture of Nelson I took on Monday when I took Mom to see him. He is brain dead. Staring at the same spot and blinking. He doesn't hear or see. He's got a huger [sic] dent on the side where the skull was removed." So far, she hadn't told us anything we didn't already know, but that wasn't her point. She was working up the guilt she wanted us to feel before she said, "Maritza told me that Patty, Susan, and you (meaning Wil) voted to keep him on the respirator. This is the result. Maritza is an idiot for not making her own decisions."

She went from blaming Maritza solely for making a decision that she didn't agree with, to making a decision that she felt others influenced her to make. Of course, she would have called Maritza a genius had she decided to do what Evelyn wanted and removed Nelson from life support.

In closing her note, she said, "She will eventually pay for all of his suffering when it is her turn."

Exhibiting a common trait of an extreme narcissist, Evelyn was historically an expert manipulator. This time, however, she could not influence anyone in the group to get her way. Her last resort was to call me. In her desperation, she sent me a text and immediately followed that up with a phone call, not giving me much of a chance to read her text. I had anticipated the conversation with her.

"I now know whose fault it is that Nelson is suffering. I know it was Patty, Wil, and Susan who decided to keep him on life support. Nelson is a vegetable and not going to recover. He is dead! It's their fault and Maritza's for listening to them."

I wasn't surprised by her emotional explosion, but knew that she was lobbying for my allegiance. She went on, "What do you think?" Before I could respond, she interjected flattery, as if to render it impossible for me not to agree with her. Alternating between the third and second person, she said, "I knew that I could call my big brother and he would understand. He is the smartest (pouring on the manipulation) one in the family, and knows how to make the right decisions. I'm surprised at Wil; I thought he was smarter than that.

I was perturbed by her harmful attacks, but not surprised. I knew that one of the many unfortunate traits of an extreme narcissist is to shame anyone who does not take care of them or take up their cause. I would have been baffled by her outburst if it weren't for my research into the traits and behavior of an extreme narcissist. I thought that I might try to calm her down by reasoning with her, normally not an effective approach when someone like her is deeply entrenched in her position. But I felt we were all hurting over Nelson's condition and wanted to be sensitive to that. Her eventual pause to take a breather opened a window of opportunity for me to answer her initial question.

"Evelyn, it's no one's fault that Nelson is the way he is. Try to see that everyone is trying to do the best thing for him under the circumstances. Not even the doctors can tell us with certainty that he is not going to recover, so how can anyone make the decision to take whatever chance he has to live away from him?"

"Yes, but he is brain dead and not going to recover."

"Look, I was part of the group that decided to give him a chance to get better. We all thought it was the right decision at the time. This is not about placing blame on anyone. None of us caused the stroke; we are just trying to give him the best possible care. Don't focus on blame, but instead on what needs to be done for him. If you gather the siblings and Maritza, and Mom, for a family meeting to decide what to do next, it will be much better than fighting and accusing anyone of causing his suffering." For a moment, I thought I was penetrating her steely demeanor, so I continued.

"If you want to blame anyone, blame Nelson for not going to the hospital quickly enough when he felt symptoms of a stroke. He might not be in this condition had he done that. It saddens me to say this, but it was irresponsible of him to delay going to get himself checked out and treated. So, let's forget about blame and let's focus on what we need to do now."

She was not at all argumentative at this point, but I could sense disappointment in her voice that I was not about to agree with her. We finished the call with my suggestion that we gather as a family to explore our options. It's been nearly two months and I have not gotten another call from her, although I speak with Susan and Wil weekly.

July 11, 2014, was Nelson's 59th birthday. Susan accompanied Mom to visit Nelson at the Village Green facility. You can imagine how heartbreaking that visit was for them, especially Mom. As if wanting to wash away the reality of his state, they took a cake to celebrate his day. Mom was a broken woman, with the excruciating anguish at the reality that her first son was withering away before her very own eyes. It was not a happy occasion. They didn't expect it to be. But it might be the last birthday Mom could spend with her son and Susan with her brother, in spite of the fact that he could not demonstrably celebrate with them. Susan, who inherited Mom's supersensitive, emotional personality, shared in her distress. The two of them somehow found the strength to take a picture with Nelson, flanking the cake that sat on a table between them. Deep down they knew, and we all knew, that it would in all likelihood be one of the last pictures we have of him.

While Susan and Mom spent some time with Nelson in their private celebration of his birthday, Evelyn chose a different manner of celebration. She is quite the opposite of Mom and Susan's sensitivity. She is much more hardhearted. She chose to post a direct message to Nelson on Facebook. When I read it, it was clear to me that her narcissistic personality disorder compelled her to use a forum to display to the world how distraught she was. It was more about 'Look at me, everyone. Look at how I am suffering.'

I found her message to be bizarre and comical, with contradictions laced throughout. Her text, with grammatical refinement, read:

"Nelson today is your birthday! Today you're 59. I am so sorry that you're going through all of this suffering. I wish there was something I could do, but there isn't. I hurt every day, especially when I have a meal, knowing that you haven't had a meal in almost five months. Someday the nightmare will be over and you will be with God. I just pray to God that all those people who contributed to your suffering will pay three times the amount that you have suffered. I love you very much! May God help you and do what is right for you! No one on this earth deserves the quality of life you are living! Forever your sister, Evelyn."

She was driven to make that post by her affliction with NPD. Being an extreme narcissist, she was incapable of showing the emotions the tragic situation deserved. She displayed, during this ordeal, many of the traits of an extreme narcissist: no compassion, no empathy, and selfishness in her refusal to understand and listen to Maritza's or anyone's reasons for keeping Nelson on life support. She had no respect for anyone's personal feelings. It was all about her and what she wanted, and she was going to post it for the world to see. Surely, she thought, the world would want to hear what she had to say and agree with her. Her tactic was to bully and harass the vulnerable—Maritza, Susan, and Mom. She could sway Mom because she was fragile and could be influenced. She saw Maritza as incapable of challenging her, so she could try to sway her. Once she saw that she could not, she brutally verbally attacked her, and even threatened to physically harm her. Susan would no longer expose herself to Evelyn's attacks, so all Evelyn could do was disparage her name as she spoke to others about her.

In deciphering her inexplicable post, I noticed that she was so fraught with anger over her inability to influence the situation in her favor that she was acting irrationally by sending cryptic messages. I am sure that Susan, Maritza, and others were hurt by it, unless they could see that they were the words of a troubled and irrational human being. How could she in the same paragraph say "no one on this earth deserves the quality of life that you are living," yet say, "I just pray to God that all those people who contributed to your suffering will pay three times the amount that you have suffered." With that "prayer" she was asking God to inflict triple the suffering she saw in Nelson onto her brother Wil, her sister Susan, and sister-in-law Maritza. How could she wish that and not be considered evil? I thought the ultimate contradiction was that she would ask God to make other human beings suffer. I knew then that she was beyond any cure.

Coincidentally, during the time of that phone call with Evelyn, I had been researching the behavior and causes of extreme narcissism for this book. Susan and I talked about my call with Evelyn. She had also seen some of the texts Evelyn sent to Maritza, and the Facebook post. I didn't expect her to simply forgive Evelyn—that would be a process. But it was important for me to have her consider that it wasn't personal. Evelyn would do the same to anyone. I sent her a document that explained the medical condition of extreme narcissism in the hope that it would help her understand both Evelyn and Nelson better. My view is that if you cannot change an extreme narcissist (and we cannot), understanding them is your best defense against their hurtful behavior.

In the case of Evelyn, it was important to understand her affliction in order to gradually modify her behavior by challenging her the way I did when I stood my ground and suggested to her Nelson's condition was not about placing blame on anyone. The flip side of managing her personality disorder is not to give her an opportunity to victimize you by keeping a safe distance. That way she is unable to get close enough to suck the life out of you.

As for Nelson, understanding that he was an extreme narcissist helped me see his hurtful behavior toward me over the years in a different light. I no longer took it personally. Once I stopped viewing it that way, and saw what he had done to me as the result of his childhood traumas, I was able to forgive him. That was when I was once again able to smile as I replayed in my mind the good times, funny times, that we shared as brothers. I told Susan and Wil of my discovery. It was refreshing and emotionally uplifting to be able to tell them that I forgave Nelson for his transgressions against me.

I said, "I know now it wasn't personal. It wasn't his fault. He had a difficult childhood, as we all did, and he developed a defense by becoming an extreme narcissist."

I will always regret that we could not see that early enough to help him when he was younger and healthier. Now, as difficult as it is, we have to try to help Evelyn. She may be beyond a cure, but it is our responsibility as a family to challenge her in the hopes of awakening her from her trance.

From left to right: me at 4 years, Evelyn at 2, and Nelson at 6 outside our Bronx apartment on Intervale Avenue.

Nelson and Morena on their wedding day.

All the siblings with mom. Top Row from L. to R.: Wil, Nelson, and me. Bottom seated from L. to R.: Evelyn, Mom, and Susan

Nelson posing in a photo he sent to Abuelo, Julio and Abuela, Domitila.

Nelson "El Cacique" during a 2010 performance on El Mediodia television show in Puerto Rico.

Nelson in Guayama, Puerto Rico before a performance.

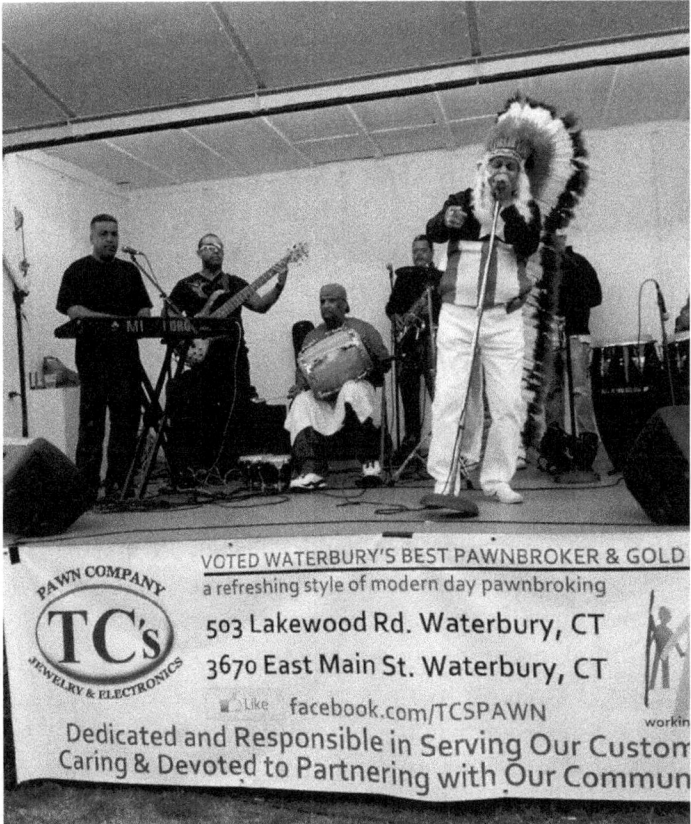

Nelson performing in Connecticut wearing his cacique attire.

CHAPTER TWENTY

Memories

One recent night, I dreamt that as I walked into the waiting room at the hospital, I saw Nelson standing by the window as if nothing had happened. I asked him how was it that he could walk, and he said, in a clear and normal voice, "I just got up and felt fine." I ran over to him and hugged him. It was as if we were kids once again, looking out for each other and being loving brothers. I woke up with tears streaming down my face, confused and sad that it was only a dream. I didn't tell anyone about that dream until now. The hardest thing for me is dealing with the notion that my brother will die soon and we will not have a chance to make peace with each other.

I don't know that we would have ever become very close again the way we were as kids. Our lives diverged quite a bit for that to happen. But we would have seen more of each other during holidays and family gatherings. I would have taken an interest in his music and possibly helped him progress in that career. I would have made sure he made a good living out of it, lending the business acumen that he was missing.

I do have good memories of Nelson and me as kids growing up in the South Bronx. Even though we lived in a dysfunctional home, when he and I were outside playing, or walking to Abuela's house on Hoe Avenue, it seems the sun was always shining. I remember that Mom dressed us for church on Sundays in white shirts and clip-on ties, fedora hats and matching trench coats in the fall. We were proud to look like miniature adults. Sometimes Mom let us go to the Episcopal Church some evenings with a family across the street, and Nelson and I went just to flirt with the girls at the church. We were perhaps twelve and ten years old. We rode in their van to the storefront church. Once there, we endured the constant singing while we played with the girls and boys who were just as disinterested in becoming church recruits as we were.

I wish that Nelson would have gone to all those Yankee games with us when Dad took me. For reasons that I only recently came to understand, he either didn't want to go, or Dad didn't want him to go. As a young kid, I was oblivious to the human dynamics that drove Nelson to dislike sports. Had things been different between them, Nelson and I could have had a great time together at the ballpark. I never saw him as anything other than my brother, not my half-brother. I never saw him as Dad's stepson. They saw things differently.

If only my parents had treated him with more care. If only Mom had recognized that he needed discipline and guidance. Perhaps it was not going to be that Dad would ever treat Nelson as his own child, since he was not. Still, there was a time when he was young enough to be saved. Tough love would have been better than no love. He could have developed into something much more than an extreme narcissist. Most importantly, we could have remained close in our relationship as brothers throughout our lives, throughout his life.

I can't help but smile when I ponder what fun we might have had if Nelson had joined Wil and me on that trip to Cancun, or dancing and drinking at the Copacabana, or having dinner at Jimmy's Bronx Cafe. No doubt he loved his Salsa music so much that he would have found his way on stage to at least introduce himself to the live act of the evening—Tito Nieves, Gilberto Santa Rosa, even Marc Anthony, or any of the many singers who appeared there. The memorable picture Wil and I had taken at the Copa one evening, with our glassy eyes from all the vodka and tonic we drank, could have included Nelson. That picture sits on my credenza in my writing office. Each time I look at it, I smile as I vividly replay that evening and think of the special bond I shared, and still share, with my brother Wil. How wonderful it would have been to feel that same sensational emotion with Nelson.

He could have sung his own songs at Janie's baptism, or at one of her birthday celebrations. He could have been with Susan, Wil, Evelyn, and Mom when we celebrated Janie's graduation from high school with a dinner at Don Pepe's Portuguese restaurant in Newark. There were too many occasions missed over the years. It seems senseless that brothers' lives could diverge so drastically that they would disappear from each other's lives for so many years, only to be reunited by the tragedy that might result in the death of one of them. I suppose I could have stood my ground when I got that call informing me that Nelson had had a stroke. I could have said, "I wish him the best, but it is not my concern." But that didn't happen. My instinct was to see him and make peace with him. If he survived, he would at least know that I forgave him. He would know that I loved him as my brother. I could then help him, encourage and support him through his strenuous rehabilitation. I am sure that would have made him happy in his most difficult time alive.

If he did not survive—something I didn't consider at first when I heard he had a stroke—I hoped that he would be able to at least hear me tell him that I forgave and loved him. He could then pass away with a peaceful heart. But I knew that many people suffer strokes and survive, so that was not something that I really anticipated. It wasn't until I heard that he did not come out of the medically induced coma that I thought he may not survive.

That's also when I began to ask how in the world Nelson got to this point. The story I got from Maritza and others was that he had been in a car accident and bumped his head. The car that collided with his left the scene of the accident. Nelson did not remember any details of the other vehicle—color, make, car or truck. This was on a Thursday evening. As the details were explained to me, Nelson was in the Emergency Room at the hospital waiting to be attended to, having been escorted by the local police who responded to the car accident. As soon as the police left after escorting him, he did not want to wait around and left. He returned home. At that time, he was not feeling any symptoms of an injury, so he didn't think of anything other than his plans for the weekend.

The next day he began to feel tired and groggy. He sat on the couch and was in a daze, unable to respond to his daughters calling his name. But that evening, he was scheduled to sing at a Valentine's Day gig in Connecticut. He did not want to cancel that performance, so he avoided going to the hospital, even though he wasn't feeling well. Apparently, at the engagement, his performance was subpar. He was slower than usual in his performance. His timing with the instrumentals was off, and the audience was not happy. His musicians, seeing that he was groggy and not his normal self, wondered if he was okay. One of them drove him home. He tripped on his way up the stairs at the front of his house. Something was very wrong. He had lost precious time and had done more harm to his brain as a result.

Who knows what might have been different had he stayed in the ER when he initially arrived Thursday evening. Would they have done a CT scan and noticed that he was experiencing the internal symptoms of a stroke? Would they have treated him that quickly and prevented further damage? I remember that Mike Ditka, the former NFL player, coach, and TV commentator, suffered a stroke last season and it was diagnosed and treated so quickly that he was able to appear at a game as a commentator the very next weekend. It was a scare, of course, but caught quickly. Perhaps that was not Nelson's fate.

When I suffered a heart attack two years ago, I woke up in the middle of the night with chest pain. It felt like heartburn, but I knew it was more than that because I was feeling nauseous, with chills, and was sweating. I didn't hesitate. I asked my wife, Estela, to call 9-1-1 right away. Within ten minutes, I was in an ambulance. The paramedics performed an EKG and confirmed that I was experiencing a heart attack. They called ahead to Somerset Medical Center, now Robert Wood Johnson, and they prepared for our arrival in the ER. Meanwhile, in the ambulance they injected me with nitroglycerin to help me until we arrived at the hospital. Once we got there, I was immediately prepared for a surgical procedure, taken up to the catheterization lab, while they waited for the cardiologist to arrive. The hospital and ambulance team performed with precision.

As they wheeled me up to the lab on a bed, I was feeling more nauseous and vomited in the elevator. Wil was by my side holding my clothing in a plastic bag, undoubtedly frightened. Estela was on her way to the hospital with our one-year-old daughter, Valentina. Once in the catheterization lab, the medical team assigned to me transferred me to another bed and hooked me up to a monitor. I could see my heart beating on the screen to my left, positioned high enough for the cardiologist to view my heart and arteries. The screen was for him, but I took a peek anyway. Wil waited outside the operating room with Estela and Valentina. It must have been frightening for them pacing outside, not knowing what was happening to me inside that room.

The surgical team performed brilliantly. Within minutes, Dr. Husain inserted a stent inside a catheter through an artery up to where my right coronary artery was 100% blocked. The instant the stent was in place, the pain I had been feeling in my chest disappeared.

I remember telling Dr. Husain that the pain had vanished. Of course, he knew that it would, having performed that procedure perhaps hundreds of times, plus he could see on the monitor that the blockage was released. He stitched the artery where he had inserted the catheter and told me to keep my right leg straight, otherwise I would pop the stitches and bleed heavily. I was transferred to the mobile bed and wheeled outside, where I could see my beloved brother, wife, and baby girl. Dr. Husain explained to them that I was going to be fine and would remain in the hospital for three days.

Dr. Husain remains my cardiologist today. I feel a special bond with him as a result of this experience. Not only did he save my life, but he is a nice man and never hesitated to take the daily calls that were part of my recovery for weeks after I left the hospital. I called him every time I felt any kind of pain in my chest. Sometimes it was a slight muscle spasm as my heart regained strength, but I didn't want to take a chance, so I would call him.

My point in all this is to say that where a person's health is concerned, hesitation can be the difference between life and death. The entire episode of my heart attack—from the time Estela called 9-1-1 to the time Dr. Husain inserted the stent—took all of thirty to forty minutes. The treatment once I arrived at the hospital took only ten or fifteen minutes. Yet, Nelson waited nearly four days from the time he was in the car accident to get treatment at the hospital. He waited two days from the time he felt actual symptoms of unusual sluggishness, altered speech, and loss of balance. That was an enormous amount of time to lose.

I can't help but think of Nelson's destiny. He hesitated to get medical treatment because he didn't want to miss an opportunity to sing before an audience. The venue was nearby, and many of his local Connecticut fans would be there. It was an opportunity for his fans to see El

Cacique, complete with his Indian chief headdress. At the same time, his decision to avoid the visit to the hospital was motivated by the impulsiveness and sense of irresponsibility that defined his life.

As Maritza, and members of his family, torment over the decision to remove him from the respirator that keeps him alive, I wonder what Nelson would do, what he would want, if he could speak or scribble a note with his own hand. He didn't have a Living Will, so we are left to guess what he would have wanted, or to believe what others say they remember him wanting done if he were faced with requiring a respirator to live. Susan and Maritza both recall that he said he did not want to be kept on life support, that he wanted to be let go. Even if that were true, it is not an easy decision for any family, and is made more difficult by the absence of concrete documentation. No one wants the monumental responsibility of ending Nelson's life, yet we all struggle with how much longer he can remain in a vegetative condition.

Still, everyone hopes for a miracle. The plan at the beginning of this ordeal, partly based on what the doctors were telling us a recovery timeframe could be, was to allow Nelson six months before considering removing him from life support. Next week we will reach that six-month milestone. It is a date, August 16, 2014, that no one is looking forward to. Some people have begun to mention a funeral service and question who would pay for it. Nelson didn't work, so he doesn't have much money saved. Maritza works, but they barely made ends meet. There was mention of four thousand dollars she had saved up from a previous car accident insurance settlement; a rather common source of income in poor neighborhoods. Then there was Evelyn's seemingly routine threatening voicemail message to Maritza, warning her this time to "watch out at the funeral because I'm going to kick your ass."

Tragedies such as this are known to bring a family together, creating a closer bond in their time of need. That is not so with our dysfunctional family. Evelyn was angry that Maritza, Wil, and Susan would not vote to remove the respirator from Nelson; Mom was angry at Susan for the same reason; Wil disengaged from the situation, though he kept communication lines open with Susan and me; and some of us were angry at our ineffectual dad, who still would not go visit Nelson—afraid he might throw up in the car. Some insisted they would not go to the funeral. All of us know that Dad will not go—absolutely abominable!

The one silver lining in all of this is that I was able to make peace with my brother. It was like the sun pushed aside the clouds after a long, heavy rain and brightened the leaves on trees. Nelson was a product of his environment. I understand why he lived his life the way he did, and I am finally okay with that. I love my brother!

EPILOGUE

At the time of the scheduled publishing of this book, Nelson remained on life support. In August, a public tribute was held in his honor at the local New Britain street fair where he performed in recent years. The organizers filled the stage with large posters of his past performances and played his songs for the large crowd of fans and well-wishers.

La Perla restaurant, one of the last venues where Nelson performed, held a fund raiser in September to help cover his medical expenses.

St. Mary's, a local Catholic church where Nelson was well known also scheduled a fund raiser in his honor.

Maritza and the family came to terms with the reality of Nelson's fate, and decided that it was time to remove him from life support.

Since Nelson was financially unprepared for emergencies, Maritza scrambled to collect the necessary funds from friends and family for the funeral service. She wanted to honor him with a two day viewing in New

Britain, allowing for his many friends and fans to pay their last respects. I was sure he would love the audience.

Sadly, on October 20, 2014, Nelson passed away at approximately 7 p.m.

Along with family members, more than two hundred friends and fans lined St. Mary's church to pay their last respects to their Taíno chief, their king. They cried, hugged, and sang his songs as he was laid to rest beside his son, Benji.

The local radio station, WPRX 1120 AM, paid tribute to Nelson with a video on YouTube where all the disc jockeys and management shared remembrances of him and said "until we meet again."

One DJ got it absolutely correct when he said that Nelson is in heaven right now organizing a new band to sing with. Now he can sing with his idol, Hector Lavoe!

Nelson Marrero, El Cacique de Puerto Rico, is finally reunited with his father and son.

Rest in Peace, my brother! Until we meet again!

For more information on NPD,
you can visit the following websites:

http://www.drsam.tv

www.psychologytoday.com/conditions/narcissistic-personality-disorder

www.mentalhealth.com/home/dx/narcissisticpersonality

To see a video of Nelson's performance on
Puerto Rico's Mediodia television show, visit:

www.youtube.com/watch?v=25l66NSbmio

www.ingramcontent.com/pod-product-compliance
Lightning Source LLC
Chambersburg PA
CBHW060851280326
41934CB00007B/997